MW01006685

Introduction to Philosophy—
Thinking and Poetizing

# Studies in Continental Thought

EDITOR
## JOHN SALLIS

CONSULTING EDITORS

Robert Bernasconi
Rudolf Bernet
John D. Caputo
David Carr
Edward S. Casey
Hubert L. Dreyfus
Don Ihde
David Farrell Krell
Lenore Langsdorf
Alphonso Lingis

William L. McBride
J. N. Mohanty
Mary Rawlinson
Tom Rockmore
Calvin O. Schrag
†Reiner Schürmann
Charles E. Scott
Thomas Sheehan
Robert Sokolowski
Bruce W. Wilshire

David Wood

Martin Heidegger

# Introduction to Philosophy—Thinking and Poetizing

Translated by
**Phillip Jacques Braunstein**

Indiana University Press
Bloomington and Indianapolis

This book is a publication of

Indiana University Press
601 North Morton Street
Bloomington, Indiana 47404-3797 USA

www.iupress.indiana.edu

*Telephone orders*   800-842-6796
*Fax orders*          812-855-7931
*Orders by e-mail*    iuporder@indiana.edu

Published in German as Martin Heidegger, *Gesamtausgabe* 50: *Einleitung in die Philosophie: Denken und Dichten,* ed. Petra Jaeger
© 1990 by Vittorio Klostermann, Frankfurt am Main
English translation © 2011 by Indiana University Press
All rights reserved

No part of this book may be reproduced or utilized in any form or by any means, electronic or mechanical, including photocopying and recording, or by any information storage and retrieval system, without permission in writing from the publisher. The Association of American University Presses' Resolution on Permissions constitutes the only exception to this prohibition.

♾ The paper used in this publication meets the minimum requirements of the American National Standard for Information Sciences—Permanence of Paper for Printed Library Materials, ANSI Z39.48-1992.

Manufactured in the United States of America

Library of Congress Cataloging-in-Publication Data

Heidegger, Martin, 1889–1976.
[Einleitung in die Philosophie—Denken und Dichten. English]
Introduction to philosophy—thinking and poetizing / Martin Heidegger ; translated by Phillip Jacques Braunstein.
    p. cm. — (Studies in Continental thought)
Includes bibliographical references.
ISBN 978-0-253-35591-1 (cloth : alk. paper) 1. Philosophy. 2. Thought and thinking. 3. Poetry. 4. Nietzsche, Friedrich Wilhelm, 1844–1900—Poetic works. I. Title.
B3279.H48E3713 2011
193—dc22
                                                      2010028523

1 2 3 4 5  16 15 14 13 12 11

# CONTENTS

Contents

The present volume comprises part of a lecture course that was announced for the 1944/1945 Winter Semester in Freiburg as an introduction to philosophy, under the title "Thinking and Poetizing." The lecture course had to be cancelled after the second session as a result of an intrusion from the National Socialist Party in the middle of November 1944. This was also Heidegger's last academic lecture as an official tenured professor. The *emeritus* professor's lecture "What is Called Thinking?" only followed seven years later, after his teaching ban was lifted.

Petra Jaeger

# Translator's Foreword

Heidegger's incomplete lecture course *Introduction to Philosophy—Thinking and Poetizing* originates from the 1944 Winter Semester at Freiburg and appears in this volume along with revisions and notes from volume 50 of the Heidegger *Gesamtausgabe*. GA 50 also contains Heidegger's undelivered lecture from 1940, *Nietzsche's Metaphysics,* which has already been published in English and is not translated here. However, a translation of Heidegger's notes to *Nietzsche's Metaphysics,* which contain several important statements regarding Heidegger's reading of Nietzsche, can be found at the back of the volume as the "Appendix to *Nietzsche's Metaphysics.*"

The 1944 lecture course *Introduction to Philosophy* opens with Heidegger clarifying that, despite the title, it is not an introduction (*Einleitung*) to philosophy. Instead, Heidegger proposes a guide (*Anleitung*) to philosophy, or more precisely, a guide to thinking, in which we will be guided by the thinker Nietzsche. And it is especially the relationship between Nietzsche's poetry and philosophy that Heidegger suggests will help guide us. To articulate his method of thinking about Nietzsche's thinking and its poetic character, Heidegger continually employs a string of German verbs formed from the word *denken* (to think): *an-denken* (to think of, to reflect), *mit-denken* (to think with), *zu-denken* (to-be-thought), and *nach-denken* (to think about). The verb *nachdenken* also implies a way to gain access to things and objects in the sense of "contemplation," and I have translated it as "to contemplate" when the context requires this more robust sense of the word. Whenever Heidegger hyphenates the verb *nachdenken* as *nach-denken,* then the parallel hyphenation results in "con-template," emphasizing the directional pursuit of the task of thinking.

Another basic word for "thinking" that Heidegger uses repeatedly in this lecture is the German word *sinnen* (to think, to meditate). *Sinnen* derives from the Old High German *sinnan*, "to clear a way." Heidegger provides an insightful etymology in *Wissenschaft und Besinnung* where he defines *sinnen* as "pursuing a path, which has already taken up a matter from itself, is in our language, *sinnan, sinnen*. Becoming involved with the meaning [*Sinn*] is the essence of *Besinnung*" (GA 7, p. 63). From this explanation, we can see that Heidegger thinks of *sinnen* as "thought that pursues a certain path," which is a difficult notion to translate into a single word in English. Professor Günter Figal has suggested that *sinnen* contains a proximity to the German words *denken* (thinking) or *meditieren* (meditating), and I have incorporated this suggestion into the translation.

Another important term in this lecture that proves difficult for a translator is *Besinnung*, which is formed from the root verb *sinnen, besinnen*, that we have just discussed. As Heidegger himself notes, the essence of *Besinnung* is the involvement with the meaning of a thoughtful wandering. I have attempted to capture this aspect of the word by rendering *Besinnung* as "reflection" and occasionally as "awareness," depending on the context. All other translation notes are included as footnotes in the text.

## Special Thanks

I would like to extend special thanks to Professor John Sallis for his advice and direction, to Professor Michael Resler for his meticulous review and consultation, to Professor Günter Figal for his illuminating suggestions, and to the teachers and staff at the Goethe Institut in Freiburg for their instruction.

Phillip Jacques Braunstein

Introduction to Philosophy—
Thinking and Poetizing

# Introduction
## Introduction to Philosophy as a Guide to Genuine Thinking[1] through the Thinker Nietzsche and the Poet Hölderlin

### §1. The Impossibility of an Intro-duction to Philosophy

Whoever plans an "introduction to Philosophy" [»*Einleitung in die Philosophie*«] presupposes that those who are to be introduced to philosophy stand initially outside of it. Philosophy itself thus counts as an area somewhere that consists of knowledge and principles, which many people might bypass throughout their lives and from which they might thus remain closed off. Although this notion of philosophy is widespread, it misses the essence of philosophy insofar as there is no such outside—separated from the human essence—that could constitute the abode of philosophy where humans would first need to proceed in order to be in philosophy.

In truth, historical humans always already stand within philosophy because they do so essentially. Therefore, strictly thought, there is no "intro-duction" [»*Ein-leitung*«] to philosophy. But how are historical humans in philosophy? It is definitely not merely by the fact that humans make use of philosophical knowledge that is handed down from somewhere. Historical humans think [*denkt an*] of the origin and future from out of these, respectively. From the horizon of such reflec-

---

1. [To avoid an explicit connection to *Being and Time*'s analysis of authenticity and inauthenticity, I have translated *eigentlich* as "genuine" in an attempt to convey the sense of the word as what is "real" or "actual."—Trans.]

1

tion [*Andenkens*], humans always think what is present. Insofar as historical humans think what has been, what comes, and what is present, they think beings as a whole according to all ways of being. If humans think that which is—and they think this constantly in some way—then humans also think and have always already thought what has been and what will come. Thinking in this way, humans already move everywhere within this thinking, which has been called "philosophy" since antiquity. As reflective humans, humans "philosophize." By moving within such thinking, humans sojourn in the region of what remains to-be-thought [*Zu-denkende*] for this thinking. What is to-be-thought and also, somehow, always already what has been thought [*Gedachte*] is the realm of the sojourn for humans insofar as they philosophize. This realm of the sojourn is philosophy.

We believe we know in which realm and space buildings stand and in which realm the trees grow. We barely think about which realm philosophy, thinking, is in and in which realm art is, and what they are. We do not even think about the fact that philosophy and art could themselves in each case be the realms of the sojourn of the human.

We are now saying: historical humans are already *in* philosophy. Humans no longer need to be introduced to philosophy. They cannot just be lead at one point into philosophy nor can they be placed into philosophy from somewhere else. But if this is true, then all humans are "philosophers," or, as we also like to say, "thinkers." In a certain way, that is what they are. The human among all beings is that being that thinks. The human is the thinking being. Therefore and only therefore can and must there be thinking ones in a distinguished sense among humans, which we call "the thinkers." Therefore and simply for this reason, there is also thoughtlessness only among humans, which continually has its root in a loss of reflection [*Besinnunglosigkeit*].

## §2. The Need for a Guide to Become at Home in Genuine Thinking

According to what was said, philosophizing is thinking, and all thinking is already, somehow, a philosophizing. Philosophy belongs, in a way that remains to be determined more closely, to that region itself within which the human *as* the reflective-thinking being [*das andenkend-denkende Wesen*] sojourns. Yet humans can truly be at home or not at home in this place where they sojourn according to their essence. Dwelling [*Wohnen*] is what we call the native sojourning in the realms in which the human belongs. In this way, to be sure, historical humans continually sojourn in philosophy, but are only rarely at home in it. They do not dwell in it. Therefore, there is need of a guide [*Anleitung*] to become at home in philosophy. Through this guiding, our thinking, which is not always at home [*zuhause*] in what is its most own, learns to dwell and thus becomes a more genuine [*eigentlicheres*] thinking. The guide to thinking need only insure that we who are already the thinking ones become more thoughtful. Thus, the acquisition of philosophy, properly understood, never entails the frequently arduous and fruitless memorization of strange concepts and doctrines that we will one day forget again.

We should in no way abandon immediate daily thinking through the guide to philosophy; instead, we, the thinking beings, should become more thoughtful in this daily thinking, which means that we should become more contemplative [*nachdenklicher*] and more reflective [*andenkender*], and thereby, learn to genuinely [*eigentlich*] think. Philosophy is not, however, what it widely and continually appears to be: the remote or the beyond of "real" life. Rather, philosophy as genuine thinking is the continually unknown region in which habitual thinking constantly sojourns without becoming versed or at home in it as the property [*Eigentum*] that has been allocated to the essence of humans insofar as they are the thinking ones.

----

## §3. The Manifold Ways for a Guide to Genuine Thinking. The Question: "What Now Is?"

Yet just as the ways and sojourns of daily thinking are diverse and diversely directed, so too are the possibilities that stand open for a guide to philosophy.

We are constantly and everywhere thinking that which is, even if we are only rarely aware of this thinking. Therefore, we often only fleetingly grasp that which is. We barely have an understanding of the way of being in which beings, so diversely spoken of and compelled [*betriebene*], show themselves to us. When we ask the simple question: "what now is?" [*Was ist jetzt?*], then the answers to this question could hardly be reviewed and counted. For, the question is already ambiguous despite its simplicity. The confusing multiplicity of the answers corresponds to this question's ambiguity. We ask, "what now is?" As long as we do not thoughtlessly recite the question, the preliminary question already becomes necessary: "What does 'now' mean here?" Do we mean this "moment," this hour, this day, today? How far does today reach? By today, do we mean the "present-time" [*Jetzt-Zeit*]? How far does this extend? Do we mean the twentieth century? What would this be without the nineteenth century? Does the "present-time" mean the entire modern era [*Neuzeit*]? Does the question, "what now is?" ask about what "is" in *this* time, the modern era?

What do we mean by "is?" *Is* it and does it count as the beings that can appear before us as tangibly available? Or do these beings ever remain only a fleeting appearance of what "really" "is" in the background and has being? What does one generally mean today, in the current time, and in the modern era, by "being"?

Beings are the real [*Wirkliche*] which are accessible to reification. Being, then, means reality [*Wirklichkeit*], objectivity [*Gegenständlichkeit*]. But what does reality mean? In what sense is realization [*das Wirken*] meant? What does objectivity mean? Who objectifies what? By what right does the objective [*das Gegenständliche*] precisely count as that which is? Depending on the sense in which we understand the "now" and the "is" and depending on the clarity, thoroughness, and reflectiveness [*Besinnlichkeit*] with which we think that which has been understood, the answer to the question "what now is?" will turn out differently. Nonetheless, the many irreconcilable answers can be brought to agreement as soon as we are able to think the mentioned questions from out of genuine thinking.

## §4. The Consideration of Thinking in its Relation to Poetizing as One of the Ways for a Guide to Genuine Thinking.

### Nietzsche and Hölderlin

At this stage of genuine thinking, only those can guide us, of course, who already genuinely think. Thinking in such a way, they already are saying to us in advance and have already said what now is. They are the thinkers and poets.

Why do we suddenly name the poets as well, when after all, we are dealing with thinking? Are the poets actually thinkers? Are thinkers fundamentally poets? By what right do we like to name them, thinkers and poets, in the same breath? Is there a distinct yet still concealed relationship between both of them in their essence? Does the relation of both consist in the fact that thinking is a meditation [*Sinnen*] just as poetizing?

Part of what is peculiar to the thinker and the poet is that they receive their meditation [*Sinnen*] from the word and shelter it in saying, such that thinkers and poets are the genuine preservers of the word in language. Then thinking, just as much as poetizing, always has its distinction in the fact that they are always a saying and a meditation [*Sinnen*] wherein the awareness [*Besinnung*] of what is, is expressed in language. If it were otherwise, then we would lack the reason for why we like to mention thinking and poetizing, philosophy and poetry, together in the expression "thinkers and poets." This happens to us almost automatically. We are touched and attracted by a vaguely intuited connection between the two.

Maybe we still recall [*entsinnen*] that we "are called" the people [*das Volk*] of poets and thinkers. Not only are we called the people, but we also are the people.

Are we that people? Are we already [that people] by virtue of the fact that we historically affirm and announce that there have been these great thinkers and poets among the Germans?

The cohesion of thinking and poetizing seems to be so intimate that thinkers stand out at times through the poetic character of their thinking, and that poets only become poets through their nearness to the genuine thinking of thinkers. One tends to call the last thinker of Western philosophy

Friedrich Nietzsche, the "poet philosopher," and one thinks of the "poet" from *Thus Spoke Zarathustra*. One also knows that the first thinkers of Western philosophy expressed their thought [*Sinnen*] in so-called "didactic poems." Conversely, we know that the poet Hölderlin in part owes what is far-reaching, still-concealed, and all-anticipating in his thinking [*Sinnen*] to a unique nearness to philosophy, a nearness which we otherwise do not encounter anywhere in this form, as long as we exclude the poets of the Greeks, Pindar and Sophocles, with whom Hölderlin lived in a constant dialogue.

The title of the lecture *Introduction to Philosophy* also bears the subtitle, *Thinking and Poetizing*. As was said earlier, many ways stand open for the attempt at a guide to genuine thinking. One of the ways is to consider thinking in its relation to poetizing and to call attention to the relationship between thinking and poetizing. *This* way in turn offers many kinds of outlooks and thus many possible perspectives. In general, beginning a discussion about thinking and poetizing by seemingly not having any visible foothold could lead us quickly into groundlessness and fruitlessness.

But what would it be like if we were to look for poetizing and thinking where they encounter us at a peculiar necessity of their historical interrelation, that is to say with Nietzsche who as a thinker is a poet, and with Hölderlin who as a poet is a thinker? Both *are* both in a distinguished reciprocal relationship between thinking and poetizing. Yet this interrelation is characterized and rooted completely differently in Nietzsche's thinking and in Hölderlin's poetizing.

With both names, moreover, we name a thinker and a poet who immediately concern our age in a still barely transparent way because they presumably go beyond us, each in a different way. Nietzsche and Hölderlin are then not just arbitrary examples [*Beispiele*] of a special interplay [*Zusammenspiel*] between thinking and poetizing. For some time now, it has also become common to mention Hölderlin and Nietzsche together, regardless of what motivations determine this naming, apart from whether Nietzsche's thinking distinguishes itself appropriately from Hölderlin's poetizing. But the very fact that Hölderlin and Nietzsche are named together in such an emphasized way indicates that we stand in an essential relation to them.

This poet Hölderlin and this thinker Nietzsche historically concern us in a special way, even when we barely take notice of them or even if we know them only from our education. If we substitute the undetermined title "Thinking and Poetizing" with the names Nietzsche and Hölderlin, then the relationship between thinking and poetizing and the question concerning the relationship of both of them become historical and binding for us in a manifold sense. Both names, Nietzsche and Hölderlin, are here intentionally not named according to the well-known historical succession. The reason for this procedure will be obvious later. First, we will pay attention to Nietzsche's thinking.

If we attempt to think about Nietzsche's thinking, we are forced to contemplate what was thought by him, i.e., what was to-be-thought for him. We are at once necessitated to think *that which now is* with Nietzsche as the last thinker of the modern era. This last thinker of the modern era is the European thinker who thinks the modern essence of the West simultaneously with the historical essence of the modern world history of the globe. If Nietzsche thinks what *is*, and thereby attempts to say what beings as a whole actually are with respect to their being, then Nietzsche says: all beings are, insofar as they are, will to power. But will and willing are always a becoming. However, since becoming as such also "is," the question arises as to what being [*Sein*] is proper [*eignet*] to the will to power as the becoming of everything. Even though the fundamental trait of all beings in their being appears in the will to power according to Nietzsche, the being-character of this being [*Seinscharakter dieses Seins*] still remains undetermined and un-thought whenever we are merely content with saying: all beings are will to power.

Now, exactly to what extent this thinking—which thinks all beings as will to power and expresses its main thought with this verbal framework—should have a distinguished nearness to poetizing is initially difficult to see. What does poetry have to do in the realm of the will to power? Or, is that which we call "poetizing" not everywhere of the same essence? To what extent poetizing becomes essential for Nietzsche's thinking in an emphasized way, why this thinker must "poetize" the figure of "Zarathustra," and what especially this poetizing means within his thinking; all of this we can only clarify if we experience

Nietzsche's thinking as the genuine European-planetary thinking. After all, one already thinks along with and thus affirms Nietzsche's thinking wherever his "philosophy" is rejected and condemned, according to loudly declared assurances. To what extent these rejections merely hit upon an imaginary shape and how frequently the affirmations do so is a question in itself. Before addressing this, it would first be necessary to ask if it is even possible to reject an essential thinking. This peculiar behavior is presumably a self-delusion.

The European-planetary trait in Nietzsche's metaphysics is itself, however, only the consequence of that fundamental trait of his philosophy through which his philosophy reaches back— almost against his knowledge [*Wissen*] —into the concealed destiny of Western thinking, and in a certain way completes its determination. So long as we do not consider this fundamental trait of the thinking of the last modern thinker, the confrontation with Nietzsche has *still not begun*.

---

§5. The Confrontation with Thinking that
Encounters us Historically: Nietzsche's Main and
Fundamental Thought

In a confrontation [*Auseinandersetzung*], thought that speaks to us sets itself up over against our own thinking. Perhaps, with this stepping apart from each other [*Auseinandertreten*], the space [*Abstand*] is formed out of which there might come to fruition an appreciation of what characterizes the essentiality and unreachable strength of the thought that encounters us. The real confrontation does not feel out weaknesses and mistakes; it does not criticize, but rather brings the thinking that encounters us historically before our thinking and into the open space [*Freie*] of a decision, which becomes inevitable through the encounter. Therefore, we cannot con-template [*nach-denken*] Nietzsche's (or any other thinker's) thought that encounters us historically through any other path than that of confrontation. Through this confrontation, we ourselves are first drawn into the fundamental trait of the thinking that encounters historically, in order to respond to it historically.

Were the poetic quality in Nietzsche's thinking not merely to be an accompaniment, contingent on the personal predisposition of the thinker and an adornment to his philosophy; were the poetizing essence to be grounded in the fundamental trait of this thinking, then it would be necessary beforehand to recognize and contemplate the fundamental trait of this thinking, i.e., Nietzsche's fundamental thought.

Nietzsche's main thought is expressed in his doctrine of the will to power. Nevertheless, this main thought is not yet the fundamental thought of his thinking. This main thought still does not express the to-be-thought, which Nietzsche names with his own phrase "the" thought of thoughts. The fundamental thought of his thinking conceals itself in Nietzsche's doctrine of "the eternal return of the same." This thought is first thought in the thinking that poetizes the figure of Zarathustra, or more specifically, immediately prepares this poetizing. If we pay attention to this, then it is no stretch to suppose that the doctrine of the eternal return of the same is something poetized [Gedichtetes] or something merely invented [Erdichtetes]. In his much-read book about Nietzsche, Ernst Bertram calls the doctrine of the eternal return—which Nietzsche claimed to be "the thought of thoughts"—"this deceptively aping, crazy mystery of the later Nietzsche."[2] Here we must briefly note that this doctrine does not merely stem from the later Nietzsche but rather is already thought out and laid out in total clarity and scope prior to the articulation and configuration of the main thought and before the doctrine of the will to power. Whether or not one may dispense with the thought of the eternal return of the same as a "crazy mystery," and by doing so devaluate it as inane and expendable for Nietzsche's philosophy as a whole, depends on the decision of whether and how Nietzsche's teaching of the eternal return of the same goes together with his teaching of the will to power. However, this decision can only be made if one first asks what the fundamental thought and the main thought think in Nietzsche's thinking. It remains to be asked whether this distinction between the fundamental thought and the main thought is only

2. Ernst Bertram, *Nietzsche: Versuch einer Mythologie* (Berlin, 1918; 2nd edition 1919), p. 12.

necessary in relation to Nietzsche's philosophy, or whether this distinction conceals a relationship that characterizes all of metaphysics as such and that thereby comes to light in a special way in the era of the completion of metaphysics. These questions have never been asked at all, let alone sufficiently answered. The discussion of these questions is the touchstone on which every interpretation of Nietzsche's philosophy must prove itself. But the arbitrariness and negligence in the interpretation and assimilation of Nietzsche's philosophy have meanwhile thrived to such an extent that one can dare to praise the doctrine of the will to power as the greatest insight and in the same breath dismiss the doctrine of the eternal return of the same as Nietzsche's temporary private "religious" opinion.

So long as the confrontation with Nietzsche's thinking remains in such a terrible state, every position on this philosophy, whether it results in affirmation, negation, or mediation, is necessarily untenable. So long as this thinking remains opaque for us with respect to the interior relationship of his fundamental thought and his main thought, we may not claim to know this thinking as a thinking. Yet if this is the case, how are we to find out whether and exactly how *poetizing* is essential in this *thinking,* such that we can speak of the thinker Nietzsche as the poet of "Zarathustra"?

If we prepare ourselves for a guide into genuine thinking by attempting to give a few indications [*Hinweise*] of thinking and poetizing, then this indicating [*das Hinweisen*] can only happen on the path of a confrontational setting-apart [*Auseinander-setzung*], which brings the thinker who concerns us and the poet who concerns us to language in his own saying. We speak of indicating. That should imply that what is attempted here is limited in many respects and is content to call attention to something essential.

First of all, it is a matter of following the thinker Nietzsche in the thinking of his fundamental thought, in order to become ready for treading the path that the fundamental thought shows us. On this path, we will be torn out of our normal, everyday thinking and initially and frequently, for a long time, will be placed into the indeterminate, such that we barely possess a reference through which to withstand the encounter of the thinking that concerns us. Therefore, it might do us well to pay attention to a few conditions that pertain to every attempt to think about the thinking of a thinker.

---

## Review (First Draft)

Philosophy is the thinking of thinkers. They think that which is. But even in general, humans always think that which is, although usually ineptly and imprecisely and slightly forgetfully. Humans are the ones who think but not always because of this are they also thinkers. The thinking of thinkers we call *thinking;* this word is said strictly for this. As humans always already think that which is, they constantly philosophize. Humans are already *in* philosophy. That is why humans cannot just be led "into it" [»*in sie hinein*« *geleitet werden*]. Rather, a guide [*Anleitung*] is required in order for humans to become more at home and to learn genuine dwelling where they always already sojourn, although ineptly and unadvisedly.

Philosophy is neither material for the classroom nor a field of knowledge that lies somewhere outside of the essentially human being. Philosophy is *around* humans day and night like the sky and the earth, almost even closer than they are, like the brightness that rests between them, which humans almost always overlook since they are only busy with what appears to them *within* the brightness. Sometimes, whenever it darkens, humans become especially attentive to the brightness around them. But even then, humans do not pay closer attention to it, because they are accustomed to the fact that the brightness returns.

The guide to thinking strives *for* it to become *brighter* around us, and for us to become more circumspect of the brightness. In this manner, we will perhaps become more thoughtful as the thinking ones that we already are. Since thinking thinks that which is, beings must become more existent [*seiender*] in order for us to be more thoughtful. But how do beings become more existent, or also more nonexistent [*unseiender*]? That depends on being itself and on how being sends itself to the human.[3]

---

3. [Heidegger uses the verb construction *sich schicken* which also could be read, "how being becomes appropriate to the human."—Trans.]

Many ways are open for a guide to thinking. This lecture bears the title "Thinking and Poetizing." Usually we say "poetizing and thinking" in the reverse order, according to talk of "poets and thinkers," talk that affects us in a peculiar way. Occasionally one hears someone say that we are "the people [*Volk*] of poets and thinkers." When foreigners say this, they mean that we are the people who primarily produce poets and thinkers, while they produce machines and fuels. All too often, following these foreigners, we opine the same as they do. However, that we are the people of thinkers and poets—and we are it and will be it—does not mean that we produce [*hervorbringen*] thinkers and poets as figures for displays of culture; rather, it means that our thinkers and poets produce [*hervorbringen*] us in our essence. The question remains as to whether we are essentially still great and noble enough to let ourselves be brought forth [*hervorbringen zu lassen*] into our essence, regardless of what foreigners say about us. For they believe that as long as we simply behave and produce good thinkers and poets, they can remain undisturbed in their own engagements. This is another, even greater error. After all, it could and will one day certainly be the case that our thinking and poetizing disturbs the foreigners—not in their engagements, to be sure, but in their essence—and makes them uncertain [*fragwürdig*], bringing them to the verge of reflection [*Besinnung*].

Yet even here, the question at first emerges of whether and how we ourselves will protect our historical determination, even when the path of history—upon which the historical determination becomes our destiny—still remains so concealed.

The title of the lecture thematizes "thinking and poetizing." We are therefore paying attention to discussions "about" thinking and poetizing precisely by means of a comparison of both. By distinguishing thinking from poetizing, thinking steps out into its essence more sharply.

Surely, if we only talk about thinking and poetizing in general, everything easily loses itself in the indeterminate and vacuous. For this reason, we are thematizing the thinking of a determinate thinker and the poetizing of a determinate poet. We can clarify the title "Thinking and Poetizing" with the contraposition of the names Nietzsche and Hölderlin. But why not Kant and Goethe? The lecture itself will provide the answer to this question. May we simply note for now, extrinsically, that Nietzsche is that thinker who thinks what now is. Hölderlin is that poet who poetizes what now is. Nonetheless, what Nietzsche thinks remains infinitely distinct from what Hölderlin poetizes. But is it not supposedly the same what the one thinks and the other poetizes? Is it not supposedly that which is? Then there would have to be an infinite difference concealed in that which is, i.e., in "being" itself.

There will also be reasons why Nietzsche, the thinker, is a poet in his own way and why Hölderlin, the poet, is a thinker in his own way. In Nietzsche and Hölderlin's thinking and poetizing, poetizing and thinking are interwoven with one another in a single and wondrous way, if not completely joined together [*verfügt*].

It still preliminarily looks as if we ought to be dealing with matters "about" Nietzsche's thinking and "about" Hölderlin's poetizing. Pursuing this method of comparing them historically, we could certainly report many interesting matters. But this historical reasoning can never become a guide to thinking. This guide demands that we think with [*mitdenken*] the thinker and poetize with [*mitdichten*] the poet. For this it is necessary that we pursue the thinker by thinking [*nachdenken*] and pursue the poet by poetizing [*nachdichten*].[4] Only in this way will we experience what relation exists with the vacuous [*nichtssagenden*] "and" that stands between Nietzsche "and" Hölderlin, that stands between this thinker *and* this poet, which now and in the future stands between thinking and poetizing.

We faithfully think along with Nietzsche's thinking if and only if we contemplate the thought which the thinker himself calls "the thought of thoughts." That is the thought of "the eternal return of the same." In the thinking of this thought, Nietzsche poetized the figure of Zarathustra. Nowhere else, and at no previous time has a figure been poetized within the thinking of Western metaphysics. This only becomes necessary within the completion of modern metaphysics and of metaphysics in

4. [Grimm's dictionary notes that *nachdichten* is a synonym for *nachdenken*. *Nachdichten* can also mean to poetically imitate another poet; and *Wahrig* dictionary notes that *nachdichten* can also be a *translation* of a poem or epic.—Trans.]

general. The fact that this poetizing becomes necessary is the *sign* of the completion of Western metaphysics. Only at one other time is thinking poetized in metaphysics, albeit differently, i.e., precisely in the beginning of Western metaphysics in Plato's thinking. Plato poetizes his "myths." What this poetizing here and there is within thinking, and whether these thinkers are thereby poets or remain thinkers, is something we must ask in due time.

# Chapter One
## The Fundamental Experience and Fundamental Attunement of Nietzsche's Thinking

### §6. The Godlessness and Worldlessness of the Modern Human as Nietzsche's Fundamental Experience

The thinking of a thinker is true [*wahr*] if it guards [*wahrt*] the advent of being. Thinking guards being by tending being's advent thoughtfully in its saying, by sheltering [*birgt*] being in the word of the saying, and at the same time thereby concealing [*verbirgt*] being in language. This thoughtful guarding [*andenkende Wahren*] of being is the true-ness [*Wahr-heit*] of philosophy.

Every true philosophy is therefore, in its exterior form, an answer to the question that is asked at every point in time of the human's historical existence [*Daseins*]. This question may at times remain unexpressed. It can hide itself in different versions and circumlocutions to the point of being unrecognizable. However, it can be reduced everywhere and without forcefulness to the simple formula: What now is? All thinkers ask in their time about that which is.

This question of thinking emerges in an experience through which thinking is determined by what prevails as the "ground" [*»Grund«*] of that which is. Every thinking rests on a fundamental-experience [*Grund-erfahrung*]. What de-termines [*bestimmt*] thinking pervasively attunes [*durchstimmt*] it at the same time in its origin and breadth. All thinking resonates within a fundamental-attunement [*Grund-stimmung*].

So long as we are not experienced with the fundamental experience of a thinker and are not attuned to his fundamental attunement; so long as we do not fundamentally consider both of these in a constantly more originary way; until then, every attempt to think with [*mitdenken*] the thinking of a thinker remains futile.

However, the fundamental experience of a thinker cannot be communicated in passing by a title. A name that would designate the fundamental attunement suffices equally little. On the other hand, however, a thinker's appropriate aphorisms can serve to indicate in advance [*vorzudeuten*] the fundamental experience and the fundamental attunement of his thinking.

The fundamental experience and fundamental attunement in which Nietzsche thinks that which is may be indicated with the citation of two aphorisms. Yet since according to Nietzsche's own statement, philosophers "are thrown far ahead because the attention of contemporaries slowly turns toward them at first," Nietzsche's aphorisms tell us very little until we have interpreted them ourselves in an adequately indicative [*vordeutend*] fashion.

To be sure, one takes Nietzsche's writings as though they could be easily understood and were written for immediate household use, as though anyone could read around in them and look up any number of sayings according to their needs. But this appearance [*Schein*] of ease and superficiality is the real difficulty in this philosophy, since this appearance, through the impressionable and charming quality of its language, seduces us into forgetting the thought. We do not reflect [*besinnen*] any further about the realms out of which the thinker actually speaks, or into which region of the human's sojourn the thinker speaks. We consider to an even lesser extent that the innermost destiny of the history of the West is expressed in Nietzsche's thinking. We are not aware that, through what is spoken in this thoughtful word, we are already moved [*versetzt*] into the confrontational setting-apart [*Aus-einander-Setzung*] with him, whether we take this burden upon ourselves or let it lie there, and consequently stumble about in a confusion of mere opinions.

However, if we attempt to exert ourselves differently, then we must *never* remain at a fixed interpretation. For all genuine thinking and thinking-along with a thinker is a wandering, indeed the wandering into that which, as the simple, lies near. Experience only exists in such wandering. Only in experience do we become more experienced. The quiet gathering toward what is essential only emerges with increasing experiencedness [*Erfahrenheit*].

### a) The "Creation" of the Gods by Humans

The *one phrase* that can indicate Nietzsche's fundamental experience and fundamental attunement to us reads: "Almost two thousand years and not a single new god!" (vol. VIII, pp. 235–36). Nietzsche wrote this aphorism in the fall of 1888, just a few months before the outbreak of his insanity, when he was at the point of presenting his philosophy as a whole according to a new plan. The title of the planned work reads: *Revaluation of all Values.* It was to consist of four books. Nietzsche only succeeded in writing the first book in just a few weeks. It is titled: *The Antichrist: Attempt at a Critique of Christianity.* The second book is titled: *The Free Spirit: Critique of Philosophy as a Nihilistic Activity.* The title of the third book is: *The Immoralist: Critique of the most Catastrophic Kind of Ignorance, Morality.* The fourth book, which was to affirmatively present Nietzsche's own philosophy is titled: *Dionysus: Philosophy of the Eternal Return.* The name of an Asian-Greek god shines above the last phase of the last figure of Western metaphysics.

The quoted aphorism, "Almost two thousand years and not a single new god!" comes from the first book, *The Antichrist.* This phrase does not just say what Nietzsche so often previously expressed, "God is dead"; rather, it says that Europe has been unable for two thousand years to create a new god. For, this is an essential thought of Nietzsche's: that the gods are "created" by humans. They are "created" according to the respective "religious ability" [*Begabung*] of peoples. The following sentences precede Nietzsche's aphorism:

> The fact that the strong races of Northern Europe have not pushed away the Christian God does not speak well of their religious ability, not to mention their taste. They *ought* to have dealt with such

a sick and decrepit monster of *décadence* {which according to Nietzsche's opinion is the Christian God}. But that is a curse upon them since they have not dealt with the Christian God: they have adopted the sickness, the old age, the contradiction into all their instincts—they have not *created* a god since then![1]

The last word "created" is underscored because it expresses one of Nietzsche's essential thoughts. The God and the gods are a "product" [*Erzeugnis*] of the human.

We are here at the point, from an allegedly superior knowledge that naturally does not reach very far, to critically ask whether a God, conceived as a human product, could actually be a God. We could also ask something else, namely, what a "religious ability" is supposed to be if it, as "religious," is not already based on the divine and is already claimed by the divine through a God, and only by this claim becomes "religious," provided that the "religious" is allowed to be stamped as a matter of "ability," and also assuming that "the religious" is that realm in which one can simply speak of the God and the gods at any time. For, the "religious" is not just nominally "Roman." The Greeks had no "religion" because they were and still are the ones looked at [*Angeblickten*] by the gods.

These and other considerations about the creation of the gods, about "the religious ability" and about religion itself, propounded at the right time and at the right place, may have their place. Yet initially these considerations are hasty and easily rush us, who are propounding them, into an area that knows no bounds and thereby removes us from a confrontation with what needs to be thought here.

For prior to that, we have to take notice of a twofold issue: first, the scope of the thought of the human as the "creating one" and of the "creative" in the human; second, the historical origin, and that is also the "metaphysical" foundation of the thought.

1. [All translations of Heidegger's citations of Nietzsche and Hölderlin are my own. Whenever previously translated versions of the passages were available, I have compared them with mine. And note: braces indicate Heidegger's insertions, whereas square brackets indicate translator's or editors insertions throughout.—Trans.]

### b) The Scope of the Thought of the Human as the "Creating One," the "Creative" in the Human

For Nietzsche, not only are the gods and God human "products," but everything that is. We gather this from one of Nietzsche's notes from the year 1888. It is in a place where it is rarely found, where it does not belong in the first place, and definitely not in the manner in which it stands there. It is in the book compiled by Nietzsche's sister and Peter Gast, which one knows by the title *The Will to Power,* where it was appended completely arbitrarily and thoughtlessly as a preface to the first part of the second book; and it is even inserted without any numbering, which is otherwise provided for all the other pieces gathered together for the production of this fateful book. The note, whose illuminating scope in regard to the leading theme of the lecture is easily recognizable, reads as follows:

> All beauty and sublimity that we have lent to real and imaginary things, I want to take back as the property and product of the human: as the human's most beautiful apology. The human as poet, as thinker, as God, as love, as power—oh its royal generosity with which it has endowed to things in order to *impoverish* itself and to make *itself* feel miserable! That was up to now its greatest selflessness so that it was amazed and worshiped and knew how to hide from itself that *it* was the one who had created all that it admired. (*Der Wille zur Macht,* vol. XV, p. 241)

It is clearly said here: the human as poet, as thinker, as God, as love, and finally as power. The word "power" is named last out of clear thinking, as "power" for Nietzsche is always will to power. Will to power, however, is poetizing, thinking, the godhead of the God. For Nietzsche, "will to power" is also love. The human *is* all of this insofar as [the human] stands in a distinguished way within the will to power. Everything that is, is loaned and lent by the human and carries its forms: μορφὴ τοῦ ἀνθρώπου.

Everything that is, is one single anthropomorphism. The human is "*the* creator" in it. "The creative" is the essence of the human. If we insert a Roman word here, namely the word "genius," then we immediately recognize what else is to be considered here, namely the historical origin of anthropomorphism and its metaphysical core. In Nietzsche's note, the modern thought of the human as "genius" expresses itself with its final consequence. Genius and the creative are the indication and standard for that which obtains in truth and deserves care, i.e., that which awakens "culture" and characterizes it.

### c) The "Metaphysical" Ground of the Thought of the Creative Human: The Modern Determination of the Essence of the Human

The thought of the creative human or, stated more clearly, the thought that the human achieves its highest fulfillment in creativity and as genius, and likewise the concurrent thought of "culture" as the highest form of existence [*Daseinsform*] of the historical human, is founded on the modern determination of the essence of the human as the subject setting-itself-upon-itself, by which all "objects" are first determined as such in their objectivity [*Objektivität*].

By setting its essence upon itself, the human rises into the willing of its own self. With this up-rising [*Aufstand*] of the human into the will as the willing of itself, all things simultaneously become an object [*Gegenstand*] for the first time. The human in this up-rising and the world as object belong together. Within the world as object, the human stands in the up-rising. The up-rising human only admits the world as object. Reification [*Vergegenständlichung*] is now the fundamental comportment toward the world. The innermost and today still-concealed essence of the reification, not its consequence or even just its mode of expression, is technology.

The up-rising of the modern human to reification is the metaphysical origin of the history of the modern human, in the course of which the human binds its essence ever more univocally in the absolute fact that [the human] is the creating one.

By virtue of this, namely that the modern human wills itself as the "creating one," two developments are decided here that correspond to each other and thus belong together: the creating one in the sense of the creatively active, and the creating one in the sense of the worker. The same era that accomplished the transformation of the human essence to subjectivity, the Renaissance, then carried this human essence back into the Roman and Greek age as the human image. Since then, one views the poets and the thinkers, the artists and the statesmen of the Greeks as "creative" humans, an idea which is as un-Greek as hardly any other of the ideas still circulating, with the exception of the corresponding opinion of the nineteenth century, that the Greeks were a "culture-creating" people. If the Greeks had spent their time creating a "culture," then they would never have become who they are.

### d) Ποιεῖν Thought in a Greek Way

But how can we claim that the idea of the creative and creating human is foreign to the Greek essence? Do not even the Greeks call poetizing by the name ποιεῖν, ποίησις, determinations according to which we still today say "poesy" [*Poesie*] instead of "poetry" [*Dichtung*]? But what does ποιεῖν mean? According to the dictionary, it literally means "making" [*machen*]. But what is making, particularly thought as ποιεῖν, i.e., understood in a Greek way? Do the Greeks think of "creating" in the sense of the creative producer, in the sense of the worker, or in the sense of the unity of both meanings? *Never.* What then do ποιεῖν and ποίησις mean?

We think ποιεῖν in a Greek way when we think it—precisely as what is here called the human comportment of Greek humanity toward beings—such that we thereby take the *Greek* experience of *being* as the basis, and not just any vague and unexamined idea of what is real in which we moderns, uncultivated in thinking and sufficiently confused, have been brought up. Beings, thought in a Greek way, are what are present and stand here as such in the unconcealed. Ποιεῖν is the "bringing-forth" [«*hervor-bringen*»] of something to presence into the unconcealed. We have to take our German word *hervor-bringen* completely literally at this point: "here" [»*her*«]—from out of the heretofore concealed; and "forth" [»*vor*«]—into the unconcealed, the open, which the human has before and around itself; and "bringing"—which means receiving something, administering, and giving. Ποιεῖν is this bringing-forth. We can therefore also say "pro-duce" [*her-stellen*], only when we also understand this word in the elucidated sense: positioning something as present in presence and leaving it there. In "making," precisely understood as ποιεῖν, it is not the self-enactment of an activity that is the essential by which something new is achieved. An adequate interpretation of fragment 112 of *Heraclitus* could shed some light on the real Greek meaning of the word ποιεῖν (cf. Summer Semester 1944 [GA 55, pp. 375ff.]). Every comportment that we today conceive of as "artistic creating" is for the Greeks a ποιεῖν. Poetizing is ποιεῖν, ποίησις in a distinguished sense. There prevails in ποιεῖν the taking-over of what happens to humans, the further conveyance of this occurrence, the offering-up and the setting-up. There is nothing here of the "action" [*Aktion*] of the creative spirit, and nothing of the "passion" [*Passion*] of an enraptured feeling of being overcome which then expresses itself and understands what has been expressed as testimony of one's own "cultural soul."

Ποιεῖν is the bringing of that which already "is" and that appears in what has been brought as the being that it is. That which is brought forth in the bringing-forth [*Hervor-bringen*] is not something new but is rather the ever more ancient of the ancient [*das Ältere des Alten*]. Yet whenever bringing-forth is only intent on what is always new, it abandons its own essence as ποίησις. Bringing-forth turns into the rebellious-autocratic action of the humanity of subjectivity that enjoys its life and thus attests to itself before itself. Human activity establishes itself in the capriciousness of accomplishing whatever is the newest. The Western age called modernity does not even know by which name it calls itself.

Only if we think ποιεῖν and ποίησις in a Greek way, i.e., on the basis of Ἀλήθεια, can we intimate something of the possibility according to what we call "poetizing" was thought by the Greeks as ποίησις, or "poesy." But it is also thereby indicated that we will one day have to no longer think the "poetizing" of the Greeks from our concept of "poetry" [*Dichtung*], rather from out of the essence of ποίησις, if their own word—confrontationally set apart from us—should speak to us, in place of some self-made idolatry of our own subsequent position.

This brief reference to the ποίησις of the Greeks should indicate that the character of the human *essence* in the shape of the working creative essence belongs as a distinction to the age of modernity, and only to this age. It is foreign to the pre-

ceding time, especially to the Greek age. Nonetheless, it is prepared in concealment by the metaphysics of the West that
originated in the Greek age.

### e) The Worldlessness of the Modern Human

Nietzsche's thought that the gods and all things are "products"
of the *creating* human thus expresses a destiny of the history of
the essence of the Western human. Nietzsche's thought is in no
way the exaggerated notion of measureless self-interest by some
rogue who is lost in the realm of thinking. Rather, Nietzsche's
statement that the two thousand years of Western history were
unable to "create" a new god indicates for us the fundamental
experience and fundamental attunement into which his thinking is historically placed. We merely have to supplement the
first aphorism with a second one in order that, through the cohesion of both aphorisms, we can envision the fundamental *experience* and the fundamental *attunement within this.*

The second aphorism, stemming from 1886, reads as
follows:

> Around the hero everything turns into tragedy, around the demi-
> god, everything turns into satyr play; and around God everything
> turns into—what? Perhaps into "world"? (*Jenseits von Gut und
> Böse*, vol. VII, no. 150, p. 106)

Without going into the specific content of the aphorism, we
can easily recognize the well-known fundamental conception
according to which, as expressed in the language of metaphysics, the subjectivity of the subject determines the objectivity of
the object. The hero, the demigod, and the God are thought as
subjects. Whatever stands or occurs around them regulates
itself through the way in which they respectively emerge in
their actions and suffering. What concerns us here is the last
sentence of the aphorism. There is a reason it is expressed as a
question: ". . . and around God everything turns into—what?
Perhaps into 'world'?"

The question concerns us because it concerns Nietzsche's
age. What is question-worthy [*Fragwürdige*] in this question
concerns not only the becoming of a world and how this could
happen, but prior to this it concerns the *ground* of this world-

becoming. If a God is no longer created, then how can that be created which can only exist around a God—a world? So long as humans are God-less, they must also be world-less. Thus, it is the constantly advancing, increasingly pronounced and unrelenting Godlessness and worldlessness of modern humanity that Nietzsche fundamentally experiences, such that within the horizon of what is experienced, he thinks *that* which is to be thought—for a modern thinker historically thrown into beings in this way.

## §7. The Homelessness of the Modern Human as Nietzsche's Fundamental Attunement

### a) The Loss of the Previous Home in the Anticipating and Searching for the New Home

What fundamental attunement resonates out of this fundamental experience? How do humans feel who, without God and without a world, are at the same time still supposed to be amid "beings" themselves? Without God and without a world, humans no longer have *that* in which they belong [*gehört*], to which they can listen [*hören*], whence they can be addressed [*angesprochen*] and claimed [*be-ansprucht*]. We call the circumference that is historically enclosed [*umhegten*] and nourishing [*hegenden*], that fuels all courage and releases all capacities, that surrounds the place where humans belong in the essential meaning of a claimed listening: the *home* [*die Heimat*]. The birthplace and the region of the country of birth are only the hearth of the home *if* they are already pervaded by the liberated native [*heimatlichen*] essence; [and if,] insofar as they are, they therefore give the gifts [*Gaben*] of the home that the modern human—only barely, or rarely, or too late—recognizes and tends as such. Having become God-less and world-less, the modern human is home-less. Indeed, in the absence [*Ausbleiben*] of the God and the ruin of the world, *homelessness* is especially expected of the modern historical human. Therefore, modern humans do not feel at home, and this is even and especially the case when they flee to that which makes them forget the failed home and what should replace it. But whoever, like Nietzsche, has experienced—i.e., has suffered—the Godlessness and worldlessness of the modern human, and has experienced this in a time of apparent advancement, progress, of prosperity and of new foundation—should not the fundamental attunement of homelessness have pervasively attuned this person? Indeed, it should. As it seems, we do not need to search painstakingly for the evidence of this in Nietzsche. Most of you know the often-cited poem that ends with the following stanza:

> Die Krähen schrei'n
> Und ziehen schwirren Flugs zur Stadt:
> —bald wird es schnei'n,
> Weh dem, der keine Heimat hat!

> The crows screech
> And migrate in swirling flight to the city:
> —soon it will snow,
> Woe to the one who has no home!

Here, the homelessness is even expressed poetically. However, the very fact that Nietzsche, in his manuscript, gives the poem a series of different titles indicates that this poeticized homelessness has its own distinct meaning. One title clearly reads "Without Home." The others read "Farewell"; "Out of the Winter Desert"; "The Free Spirit"; "Homesickness"; "In the German Late Fall"; "November in the North"; "The Crows"; "To the Hermit." The poem originates from the time of the writing of *Zarathustra* in 1884 (first printed in 1894). The whole poem reads as follows (vol. VIII, pp. 358-59):

| | |
|---|---|
| Die Krähen schrei'n | The crows screech |
| Und ziehen schwirren Flugs | and migrate in swirling flight |
| zur Stadt: | to the city: |
| Bald wird es schnei'n— | soon it will snow— |
| Wohl Dem, der jetzt noch— | joy to the one who still now— |
| Heimat hat! | has home! |
| | |
| Nun stehst du starr, | Now you stand numb, |
| Schaust rückwärts ach! | you look backward, oh no! |
| wie lange schon! | How long already! |
| Was bist du Narr | What have you, fool, |
| Vor Winters in die Welt | escaped before winter |
| entflohn? | into the world? |

| | |
|---|---|
| Die Welt—ein Tor | The world—a gateway |
| Zu tausend Wüsten stumm | to a thousand deserts mute |
| und kalt! | and cold! |
| Wer das verlor, | Whoever lost, what |
| Was du verlorst, macht | you lost, can stop nowhere! |
| nirgends Halt. | |
| | |
| Nun stehst du bleich, | Now you stand pale, |
| Zur Winter-Wanderschaft | cursed to the winter-journey, |
| verflucht, | |
| Dem Rauche gleich, | just like smoke, |
| Der stets nach kältern | which always searches for |
| Himmeln sucht. | colder skies. |
| | |
| Flieg', Vogel, schnarr' | Fly, bird, shriek |
| Dein Lied im Wüsten-Vogel- | Your song in the desert-bird- |
| Ton! — | tone! — |
| Versteck', du Narr, | Hide, you fool, |
| Dein blutend Herz in Eis und | Your bleeding heart in ice and |
| Hohn! | scorn! |
| | |
| Die Krähen schrei'n | The crows screech |
| Und ziehen schwirren Flugs | and migrate in swirling flight |
| zur Stadt: | to the city: |
| —bald wird es schnei'n, | —soon it will snow, |
| Weh dem, der keine Heimat | Woe to the one who has no |
| hat! | home! |

For the most part, people only know the first and last stanzas of this poem and quote them as the expression of a melancholic mood, which worries about the threatening loss of the home or mourns the loss that has in fact occurred. One ignores what is between the first and last stanza, and mishears the fundamental tone of the poem. It is ambiguous through and through. For this reason, each of the titles applies just as well as the others, such as the one called "Without Home" or another called "The Free Spirit." To be sure, homelessness is poetized in the poem, yet someone is not merely lamenting the loss of the home; here someone is speaking who at the same time finds the way in the "winter-journey" "toward cold skies." The person does not look back and no longer flees from the "winter" into the previous world, which he has completely lost and conceded in order to turn his "spirit" out into the "open." He may perhaps still have to hide what he already sees and seeks "in ice and scorn." But in this poem, a reassurance already announces itself as early as the first stanza:

> Die Krähen schrei'n
> Und ziehen schwirren Flugs zur Stadt:
> Bald wird es schnei'n—
> Wohl Dem, der jetzt noch—Heimat hat!

> The crows screech
> and migrate in swirling flight to the city:
> soon it will snow—
> joy to the one who still now—has home!

It does not say: "*a* home," but rather merely "home" in general. At the same time, the "still" concealedly means an "already": "Joy to the one who now . . ."—still over and above the ruin and loss of the previous home—already intimates home and is on the way to a new home, and no longer looks backward and never wants to go back to the previous home and to that which is still described as such. "Without Home"—that does not here mean the mere lack of home, but rather the loss of the previous one in anticipation of, and searching for, the new one. Whether this new home, thought (and that means experienced) by Nietzsche, is truly home; whether this "new" home is in the end just the final, broad residue of the old ruined home, remains another question: the question of the confrontational setting-apart. The latter will only be possible if the thinking of this thinker is finally set back into what is its own and is perceived in its full expanse.

### b) Rationality that Merely Calculates and the Forgetting of the Western Historical Determination

The manner in which this poem is cited provides good evidence for how little care is still given to the words of this thinking, when one selects and exploits them according to random "private experiences," arbitrary taste, and fluctuating moody needs. Not only are people usually just satisfied with the closing stanza instead of pondering the whole poem, but above all they overlook that a *second* poem belongs to this one, whose title reads: "*Answer.*"

This "Answer" first provides the "interpretation" of the first poem. This interpretation is a clarification and adjustment of that which can be very easily and thus not just randomly misunderstood in the first poem, insofar as one hears it as a lamentation of the one who longs for the lost home. The "Answer" reads (vol. VIII, p. 359):

| | |
|---|---|
| Daß Gott erbarm'! | May God have mercy! |
| *Der* meint, ich sehnte mich zurück | *Someone* thinks, I longed to return |
| In's deutsche Warm, | into German warmth, |
| In's dumpfe deutsche Stuben-Glück! | into the dull German sheltered-happiness! |
| | |
| Mein Freund, was hier | My friend, what here |
| Mich hemmt und hält, ist | restricts and stops me, is |
| *dein* Verstand, | *your* intelligence, |
| Mitleid mit *dir!* | Pity for *you!* |
| Mitleid mit deutschem Quer-Verstand! | Pity for German askew-intelligence! |

Does not another tone sound here? No, it is the same that sounded in the first poem, only more veiled there and thus more beautiful. The first stanza of the answer says something twofold: on the one hand, it states that the "homesickness" that announces itself in the preceding poem is not at all a yearning for something past, but rather a willing-forward into a new home; on the other hand, the stanza declares that the yearned-for-home is not the "German warmth" and the "dull German sheltered-happiness." Is Nietzsche then thinking against what is German?

Not in any way—but rather against the Germany of his own age. This is the age of the "founder years" [*Gründerjahre*], where everything groundlessly and cluelessly pursued advancement, progress, and prosperity, in order to emulate the English on a small scale and to seize a global position [*Weltstellung*] overnight. None of the prerequisites for this position were at hand, since it especially depends—here as well as in England and anywhere else—on a world that has become brittle, a world for which "Darwinism" is the only philosophy with its doctrine of the "struggle for existence" and the natural selection and choice of the stronger. Nietzsche saw this, experienced it, suffered it.

He already partially learned to see this in the elder Jacob Burck-
hardt, according to his own confession in Basel at the beginning of the 1870s.

What Nietzsche holds away from the close home of "Germany" is the non-essence [*Unwesen*] of the German that has
become powerful and that thus appears passive here, since the
Germans would have been destined, according to their essence,
to initiate out of this the reflection [*Besinnung*] on what is European and its destiny. Ever since the French Revolution and the
rise of socialism, this destiny has entered into a new stage that
is supposed to simultaneously determine a global stage. Instead
of this, looking at the whole, Nietzsche saw a mediocrity and
narrowness everywhere around him; [he saw] rationality [*Verständigkeit*] that merely calculates, which cannot envision the
great, looming historical decisions and is therefore also inca-
pable of preparing humanity and the peoples [*Völker*] for them.
That is why the second stanza states very clearly:

> My friend, what here
> restricts and stops me, is *your* intelligence [*Verstand*]

Rationality that merely calculates value and profit is the rationality of mediocrity, which still remains mediocre when it
conducts itself economically-politically on a global scale. Here,
too, a forgetting of the historical Western determination is already at work, a forgetfulness that is not compensated for by the
fact that it does itself up with opulence, morality, and demo-
cratic humanitarianism. This inability for reflection [*Besinnung*]
with broad forethought on the destiny of the history of the West
has its roots in the metaphysical age of the modern era [*Neuzeit*]
as such. Although Nietzsche could not recognize this, he nonetheless saw the inability of achieving European thought, a
thinking that extinguishes the peculiar essence [*Eigenwesen*] of
its own people so little that it in fact first raises this peculiar essence to a height in which it can outgrow itself and thus precisely be alone by itself in its own historical determination.

The "German askew-intelligence" [*deutsche Quer-Verstand*]
which, insisting on its obstinacy, never reaches the expanse of
inner superiority and therefore fails to see and does not want
to see the approaching innermost danger of history, is what

Nietzsche pities [*mit-leidet*] and helps carry, because this intelligence is merely the non-essence of a thinking that could be called upon once again to connect the torn thread of the historical tradition in the only place it can be reattached—if the West as a whole is to revisit the origins of its historical determination and reflection [*Besinnung*]—the bond with the Greeks (cf. *Der Wille zur Macht,* vol. XV, no. 419, pp. 444–45, 1885).

In a sketch for a text planned at the time, "We Philologists," the thirty-one-year-old Nietzsche writes the following in 1875:

> All history has up till now been written from the standpoint of success and that means with the assumption of reason [*Vernunft*] in success. As well as Greek history: we still have none. But the matter stands as such: where are the historians who view things without being dominated by general nonsense? I see only one, Burckhardt. Everywhere broad optimism in science . . .
> Germany has become the breeding ground for historical optimism: for that Hegel could be guilty. (vol. X, no. 254, p. 401)

Alongside *Burkhardt,* Nietzsche not only saw the Germans, but Europe altogether, fall victim to the power of rationality [*Verständigkeit*] that merely calculates in historical actions and in the contemplation of history. He saw in this rationality the rising mastery of universal mediocrity and the languor of thinking, i.e., of the human being. The following verses originate from the fall of 1884 (the *Zarathustra* period) (vol. VIII, p. 368):

| An die Jünger Darwin's | To the Disciples of Darwin |
|---|---|
| Dieser braven Engeländer²² | These dutiful Englishmen's |
| Mittelmäßige Verständer | mediocre intellects |
| | [*Verständer*] |
| Nehmt ihr als "Philosophie"? | do you take as "philosophy"? |
| Darwin neben Goethe setzen | To place Darwin next to Goethe |
| Heißt: *die Majestät verletzen*— | means: *to insult the majesty*— |
| Majestatem genii! | Majestatem genii! |

2. [Nietzsche's spelling of *Engländer* as *Engeländer* is a sardonic reference to the meaning of the country's name: *das enge Land* is "the narrow land."—Trans.]

The poem also bears the title (vol. VIII, p. 454): "To the German Donkeys." They are "donkeys" because they have abandoned their original intelligence [*Verstand*] of higher thinking for the mere rationality of average opinions. The following verses speak to this, likewise originating from the fall of 1884 (vol. VIII, p. 367):

| *Beim Anblick eines Schlafrocks* | *At the Sight of a Dressing Gown* |
|---|---|
| Kam, trotz schlumpichtem Gewande | The German, despite the frumpy robe, |
| Einst der Deutsche zu Verstande, | first came to his senses, |
| Weh, wie hat sich das gewandt! | woe, how things have shifted around! |
| Eingeknöpft in strenge Kleider, | Buttoned up in tight clothes, |
| Überließ er seinem Schneider, | he relinquished to his tailor, |
| Seinem Bismarck— | his Bismarck—intelligence! |
| den Verstand! | |

The following notes are an elucidation of these verses: *Beyond Good and Evil,* section eight: "Peoples and Fatherlands" (vol. VII, no. 253, pp. 223-24): ". . . let us finally not forget that the English at one time have already caused an entire depression of the European spirit with their profound mediocrity: that which one calls 'modern ideas' or 'the ideas of the eighteenth century' or even 'French ideas'—that which the *German* spirit has risen up against with deep disgust—was of English origin, there is no doubt."

In an earlier note from 1884 (vol. XIII, no. 872, p. 352), it says: "England's *little-minds* are the great danger now on the earth. I see more of a tendency for greatness in the feelings of the Russian nihilists than in the feelings of the English utilitarians."

However, we ourselves would become the victims of a corrupted rationality and of an increasing cluelessness and languor, if we merely wanted to see in these quotations a joke, a mockery, and an indignant insult upon the Germans and the English. We would then fail to hear the actual talking voice of the sym-*pathy* [*Mit*-leidens], a voice that, over beyond everything that is closest, narrowest, and individuated, suffers from the dark destiny of Europe's emerging history. If we, forgetting this all-deciding voice, read the words otherwise, everything becomes laughable. We then irresponsibly devalue the suffered word [*das erlittene Wort*] of the thinker. Among the notes to Nietzsche's *Thus Spoke Zarathustra* (1882–1885), we find these words:

> Concept of the higher human: who suffers from the human and not only by itself; who cannot do other than also create "the human" by itself.
>
> The suffering of the higher human is not its low point; rather, there is still something higher as its height.

Thinkers suffer upward into this height whenever they sympathize with the simple rationality that has come over the German home. In both of the connected poems, "Without Home" and "Answer," this sym-pathy, directed in two ways, speaks; it suffers back and forth between the incapacity of the previous home and the height of the future home. Therefore, the unity of both poems is expressed by a title that reads: "Pity here and there" (vol. VIII, p. 358).

Only once we carefully attend to all of this will we perhaps arrive at the fundamental attunement of that homelessness that attunes Nietzsche's thinking. This homelessness does not sink into a homesickness that yearns backward; instead it wants to go forward, i.e., away from the dullness of rationality, out into the open air of the spirit, away from the activity [*Treiben*] of a shortsighted and therefore also always short-term optimism, and into the abundant light of the realm of long decisions that concern the essence of history.

# Chapter Two
## The Creation of the New Home Out of the Will to Power

### §8. The Homeless Ones as the Conquerors and Discoverers of the New Home

The following two notes are left over from the time of the transition of 1885–1886, when much was decisive for Nietzsche's thinking insofar as he actually here began to think the thought of the will to power (vol. XIV, no. 295, p. 414):

> *We homeless ones*—yes! We want to make the most of the *advantages* of our condition, never mind perishing from it, and to let the open air and the powerful overflow of light prove advantageous for us.

The homeless ones that Nietzsche means are the willing ones, willing in the sense of the will to power, to whom the essence of their willing—wherein they will and through which they have come to be at home—appears in the abundant light of the brightest midday, and all homesickness and longing die away.

That is why in the closing stanza of the "Postlude," "From high Mountains," in *Beyond Good and Evil,* we read (vol. VII, p. 279):

Dies Lied ist aus,—der
  Sehnsucht süßer Schrei
  Erstarb im Munde:
Ein Zaubrer tat's, der,
  Freund zur rechten Stunde
Der Mittags-Freund—nein!
  fragt nicht, wer es sei—
Um Mittag war's, da wurde
  Eins zu Zwei . . . . .
Nun feiern wir, vereinten
  Siegs gewiß,
Das Fest der Feste:
Freund Zarathustra kam,
  der Gast der Gäste!
Nun lacht die Welt, der grause
  Vorhang riß,
Die Hochzeit kam für Licht .
  und Finsternis . . . .

This song is over—the
  sweet cry of longing
  died in my mouth:
A magician did it, a friend at
  the right hour,
The midday-friend—no! Do
  not ask, who it is—
it was around midday when
  one turned to two . . .
now we are celebrating,
  certain of unified victory,
the festival of festivals:
Friend Zarathustra came, the
  guest of guests!
Now the world laughs, the
  dread curtain tore,
the marriage came for light
  and darkness . . .

In the essence of willing, out of which the homeless ones will the open space [das Freie], being itself appears, which as will to power thoroughly dominates [durchherrscht] all beings. But the essence of the will emerges [steht auf] in the figure of Zarathustra. He is the highest uprising [Aufstand] of the modern essence of the human. In the figure of Zarathustra, the essence of absolute subjectivity appears for itself as the will willing itself. The human of this essence leaves the previous human behind while it discovers a new home, "new" in the sense that only now the essence of modernity comes to light and decides what is left behind as home and as the meaning of home in general for the human of the will to power. Another note that is concurrent with the previous one from 1885–1886 states (vol. XIV, no. 295, p. 414):

We homeless ones from the beginning—we have no choice, we have to be conquerors and discoverers: so that we perhaps may bequeath to our descendants what we ourselves lack—that we bequeath a home to them.

Let us pay good and long attention to this: The new home is a home bequeathed by the conquerors and discoverers; a home that the will of the "homeless ones from the beginning," and only this will, wants to create in order to entrust [*anheimzuge-ben*] the future of humanity with what has been created. In this sense of the new homeless conquerors of the home, Nietzsche says:

> In this age (where one conceives that science *is beginning*) constructing *systems*—is child's play. Rather: to grasp the lengthy decisions concerning methods, for centuries!—since the *guidance of the human future must* at least once be grasped!
> —But *Methods* that arrive out of our instincts by themselves, thus regulated habits, which already exist; e.g., exclusion of goals. (1884, vol. XIV, no. 292, p. 413)

But how, we now ask, if this homelessness itself characterizes the essence of the new home? How [would it do this] if the thinking of the thinker experiences the godlessness and worldlessness to their very core from out of the fundamental attunement of this homelessness; how, if this thinking within the "thought of thoughts" would have to think only this one thing: the grounding of homelessness as the absolute modern essence of the home?

*If* this is the case, then what was said would already be identified with the metaphysical place [*Ort*] toward which Nietzsche's thought of the eternal return of the same thinks [*hindenkt*]. Then we would immediately have to ask more fundamentally to what extent a poetizing belongs to the thinking of this thought, and in what sense of poetry this thinking itself must be a poetizing, and what truth accords with this poetizing.

Or does poetizing, especially the poetizing of the poet, not stand under the law of truth? Is it subject to the law of the beautiful, as aesthetics, i.e., metaphysics, claims? But how, and from what laws? One question leads us to another. And as long as these questions, along with the ones still not mentioned, and the more question-worthy ones are not answered, we might see that we are just groping around in the dark and are entangled in confusion when we set off on the path to contemplate Nietzsche's fundamental thought.

### §9. Nietzsche's Main Thought: The Will to Power as the *Essenz* (Essence) of Beings and as the Final Fact. The Veiled Difference between Being and Beings

In every thinker's fundamental thought [*Grundgedanken*] is thought that which gives the "ground" for what that thinker thinks. The thinker thinks that which is. The thinker thinks beings. The thinker thinks beings in the sole consideration that beings are and what they are. What beings "are," how they "are," and the fact that they "are," is what we call the being of beings. Every thinking of a thinker says what beings are, what feature pervades beings. Thinking speaks the main trait of beings in its main thought.

Nietzsche's main thought is the thought of the "will to power." In the text *Beyond Good and Evil* published in 1886, Nietzsche speaks of ". . . a world, whose *essenz* is will to power— . . ." (vol. VII, no. 186, p. 115). *Essenz* is the abbreviation for the name of a key concept in Western metaphysics: *essentia*.[1] Whenever it is asked—and the thinkers of metaphysics are continually inquiring in this way *quid est ens?*, "what are beings?"—*essentia* provides the answer to the *quid-esse* of beings. What the "world," i.e., beings as a whole, is universally in its main trait is expressed when the *essenz* is named. The *essenz* of the world is "will to power" according to Nietzsche. The word that has become standard in German for *essenz* and *essentia*, the whatness [*Wassein*], is *Wesen*. The German word *Wesen* ("essence"), which verbally means the being of beings, is immediately interpreted in the traditional sense of metaphysics, which we can better signify with the name "substance" [*Wesenheit*].

The essence [*Wesen*] of beings reveals itself to Nietzsche's thinking as will to power. Since the beginning of Western thought, an ambiguity pervades the saying of thinkers; one that is still barely experienced in its origin and import, such that they frequently say "being" instead of "beings." Speaking in this way, in which metaphysical thinking as such an-

---

1. [In order to preserve a distinction between the German words *Wesen* and *Essenz*, I have reserved the English "essence" for *Wesen* and simply left the German *Essenz* as *essenz.*—Trans.]

nounces itself, makes it seem as if the difference between beings and being were something indifferent. One can therefore also say "being" instead of "beings," without causing any damage and without being held back by anything. Yet, let us reflect [*besinnen*] for a moment: This wall "is" here. The wall is some kind of being. The wall is not, however, "being." Only because it is a being can we say: "wall." But if the wall is a being, then surely it does "have" "being." Where does it have its being? Where does this being [*dies Sein*] hide? We could enumerate and string together all the existing characteristics of the existing wall, but they would not amount to its being [*Sein*]. They cannot amount to this because the existing characteristics of the wall, and the wall as a being, already rely on the being [*Sein*] of the wall. Being is something other than beings, and yet being is not a second being beside the existing wall. Thus we hit upon the inevitable difference between beings and being but are still unable to clarify it immediately.

However, this obscurity does not just pertain to our attempted reflection [*Besinnung*] because it turned out to be too brief and remained superficial. All of Western thinking currently stands in this obscurity of the difference between beings and being. It stands in this obscurity so firmly and decisively that the thinking of thinkers has not even once become attentive to this difference itself, and specifically to its question-worthiness. Does the ground for this still barely experienced distress of thinking lie solely in the inability of thinkers, or does the ground lie in the being of beings itself? If it were so, then being itself would have up till now refused its entrance into the brightness of this difference. Presumably this is the case.

Only this should concern us initially: The veiling of the difference between being and beings that has prevailed for a long time determines the obscurity and ambiguity of the saying of thinkers, such that this vague saying of thinkers results again and again in the negligence of ordinary speaking and constantly gives it a fresh confirmation.

This indication of negligence and concern with regard to the discourse about beings and being, and thereby of the entire speaking of thinkers, has a special meaning for that thinking which, like our own thinking, attempts to think about Nietzsche's thinking. Nietzsche's thoughtful saying is distinguished by an uncommon negligence. This has broad and far-reaching metaphysical reasons, and can therefore not be remedied by a didactic correction. [The negligence] is also one of the causes that continuously increases the spreading thoughtless reading of Nietzsche's texts. No one who has not passed through the most rigorous school of thinking can con-template [*nach-denken*] Nietzsche's thinking. This thinking is not easier than Hegel's philosophy or easier than Kant's philosophy, and it is not easier than Aristotle's philosophy or Heraclitus's thinking. All thinkers are equally difficult to understand as soon as we begin to think instead of babbling and cheating ourselves by perusing the aphorisms of thinkers.

In the aforementioned passage, Nietzsche states that the *essenz* of the world is will to power; i.e., the essence [*Wesen*] of beings is will to power; or the main trait of beings, the *being* of beings, is will to power. Another note begins as follows:

If the innermost essence [*Wesen*] of being is will to power . . . (*Der Wille zur Macht*, vol. XVI, no. 693, p. 156, 1888)

According to the previously interpreted passage, being [*Sein*] itself is will to power. Now it is expressed in a conditional clause that the innermost essence [*Wesen*], and according to the previous statement, the *essenz* of being, of the will to power, is will to power. That would be a vacuous statement. The sentence, however, does say something, i.e., what Nietzsche thinks and what he said in the previous sentence, if only we substitute the negligently used expression "being" in the above-quoted sentence with the name for what is actually meant: "beings." Stated more carefully, the sentence must read: "If the innermost essence [*Wesen*] of beings is will to power"—and it is will to power according to the main principle of Nietzsche's philosophy.

A third note from 1885 (related to the sketches for the planned main work) reads: "The will to power is the final fact [*Faktum*], to which we descend" (vol. XVI, no. 8, p. 415). The will to power is "the final fact"! A Fact, something, a matter that is made and accomplished—a matter of fact [*Tatsache*]. A bridge built over the Rhine is also a matter-of-fact [*Tat-sache*]. As something that has been accomplished, a matter-of-fact is subsequently a really present matter, something existing. That

sulfur is yellow is also a matter of fact [*Tatsache*], although we
will not so easily find the doer [*Täter*] who has accomplished
this matter [*Sache*]. The factual [*das Tatsächliche*], the factical
[*Faktische*], means for us the really existent or also truly existent. If we want to reinforce that something truly is as it is said
to be, we say it is "in fact" [»*in der Tat*«] this way or "factually"
[»*tatsächlich*«] this way: "factically" [»*factisch*«] —fact [*Faktum*].
Now Nietzsche calls the will to power "the final fact"; thus the
will to power is here named as some kind of being, as that to
which we finally descend. Whither do we descend, and with
which descent and digging-down? Whenever we constantly
dig, bore, and think deeper into beings under the surface of
beings, then we will find the fact of the "will to power."

But Nietzsche does not mean to say that there are many beings within the whole world, many matters of fact, and the most
underlying matter of fact is the will to power. If thought in this
way, the will to power would just be a being under other beings,
although the one furthest underlying them. Rather, Nietzsche
intends to say that what we ultimately discover everywhere and
that therefore already pervades everything everywhere, what
beings everywhere factually are, factically, i.e., truly, is will to
power. The will to power is what beings truly are, i.e., beings according to their essence, the essence—the *essenz*—*essentia*. Nietzsche indicates this as the "final fact" in the passage just quoted.

Why should Nietzsche not use this terminology, why should
he not say "fact," for the sake of variety, instead of *essentia*?
According to the elucidation, he means the same thing in each
instance. Indeed, according to the completed "elucidation." If
we spare ourselves the elucidation and only gloss over the fact
that the will to power is at one point called the essence of beings, and then the essence of being, and then the final being
within beings, we will each time think something muddled
and confused. Or, even if we are slightly trained in thinking,
we must be shocked by this manner of Nietzsche's saying, a
shock that cannot be great enough. For in the course of Western metaphysics one difference has remained essential, and
was last thought through in an originary way by Leibniz; this
difference concerns the *essentia* and the *factum*.

A single fir tree that is really at a certain place for a certain
time is a *factum*. In contrast to this, the essence, the *essentia*, is

what we mean by "tree" in general, which determines every tree as a tree whenever and wherever it factically may be. For this reason, Leibniz differentiated two fundamental classes of truths: those that refer to the essence of beings: *veritates essentiae;* and those that refer respectively to single, actual beings: *veritates facti.* With respect to the human capacity for knowledge and the type of knowledge by which these two classes of truth are grasped, the *veritates essentiae* are also called rational truths, and the *veritates facti* are called historical truths. The word "historical" is to be understood here in the original sense of ἱστορεῖν = to investigate [*erkunden*]. The single tree only becomes accessible through an investigation, as with every *factum.* That which is essential, on the other hand, what belongs to the essence of beings, e.g., that every being is identical with itself, we will not find anywhere as a "matter of fact" [*»Tatsache«*] by investigating; rather, that is directly ascertained in the thinking of beings as such.

Nietzsche calls the will to power the essence [*Wesen*] of beings (*"essenz"*). Nietzsche calls the will to power the final fact. Those are two fundamentally different principles and different truths according to the wording and to the former traditional linguistic usage of metaphysics. In the style of metaphysical thinking, we could ask: Is Nietzsche's principle of the will to power a rational truth? Can we discover this merely by thinking that beings everywhere are will to power? Or is Nietzsche's principle a historical truth? Is it gained by way of fact-finding? Or is the principle neither an obvious truth of mere reason, nor the mere observation of a matter of fact? If the principle of beings is neither of the two, what kind of truth is suitable to it? Is the principle even demonstrable? If not, was the principle of the being of beings then just invented, fantasized [*erdichtet*], poetized [*gedichtet*] by Nietzsche? What is this poetizing, and what is it doing in thinking?

# Thinking and Poetizing
## Considerations for the Lecture[1]

### Introduction
### Thinking and Poetizing: Philosophy and Poetry
### (σοφία and ποιεῖν)

It is necessary, from out of a dire need that is barely felt, to pay attention to thinking and poetizing with a few indications.

The word "thinking," used straightforwardly, means all thinking performed by those who are called "the thinkers." Their ancient name is φιλόσοφοι, the philosophers. "Thinking" understood straightforwardly is philosophy, φιλοσοφία. To be sure, the word "poetizing" can also have an even broader meaning, and can denote as much as the following: to fantasize [*etwas erdichten*] or to invent something with the purpose of dissembling. However, we immediately understand "poetizing" rather customarily as the activity of those who are called "the poets." Poetizing, understood strictly as the art of poetry [*Dichtung*], is "poetry" [»*Poesie*«]. The word is formed from the Greek verb ποιεῖν, which means: to produce, to bring-forth. Instead of "thinking and poetizing," we could also say: "philosophy and poetry." The fact that, in the ancient names for thinking and poetizing, in the words for philosophy and poetry, two fundamental words of early, incipient Western being resound, namely σοφία and ποιεῖν (cf. Heraclitus,

---

1. [The following is translated from GA 50, pp. 136–45.—Trans.]

41

Diels-Kranz B 112), has its own reason that is largely still concealed from us.

---

## §1. The Comparing of Thinking and Poetizing. Genuine Comparing

If we take both of the word-constellations, thinking and poetizing, philosophy and poetry, as they are here presumably meant, precisely as a title for contemplation, then it immediately becomes clear that the task is to compare thinking and poetizing with one another.

We believe we know what comparing is. In comparing [*Vergleichen*], the two "things" to be compared are somehow already equated [*gleichgestellt*] with one another insofar as they are selected and presented as what is to be compared. Prior to this, there is already something the same [*Gleiches*] that is perceived about the two things, although it is mostly undetermined and evanescent. But by comparing it, it is almost as if the same were only used as a background to lift out what is different. Comparing is a method [*Verfahren*] that imposes itself everywhere upon human "thinking," most likely because it is close to thinking. Yet we still have barely thought about the reasons for which this proximity arises, from which then emerges the strange precedence, prevalence, and popularity of the comparative method.

Anything can be compared with anything, if comparing only depends on ascertaining something same and something different. The possibility of comparing in the formal sense, regardless of the "content," is limitless. We will see this easily if we just briefly consider one inappropriate possibility of comparison. Someone could, for example, compare bike-riding and poetizing. What is the same in them consists in the fact that they are both human activities. The difference appears insofar as bike-riding is a bodily activity that uses a machine, whereas poetizing is a mental [*geistig*] activity. To be sure, we occasionally hear that modern poets supposedly poetize directly on a typewriter; in this regard there would also be something the same between bike-riding and poetizing, but they would still remain different insofar as the bicycle and the typewriter are different machines. Although there could still be a lot to discover about what is the same and different in bike-riding and poetizing, we are averse to this comparison. Why? Because bike-riding and poetizing lie too far apart from each other. Comparing them is decisively unfruitful, even if it were to be carried out in much further detail.

Even if someone were still to accept this unfruitfulness, there remains in this comparison—which is somehow always already an equation—a devaluation of poetizing, even if we recognize bike-riding as a good activity. Precisely because the possibility of comparing is limitless, there always lies in the approach to the comparison a decision about what is the same—a decision that is deliberate and aware or unknowing and unaware. The things compared are set into this same from which they are viewed. For this reason, genuine comparing is always more than just comparing.

After all, comparing is not supposed to result only in the determination of what is the same and different; rather, with real comparison, we aspire to see what is different through the same and through the difference of the same to always see into the very essence of that which stands in the comparison. All comparing implicitly strives for this, but only seldom reaches it. Comparing and comparing is not universally the same.[2] The comparison of poetizing with bike-riding not only yields too little since they lie too far apart from one another, but the comparison, if it were attempted, would be a case of complete lack of taste, if not something even worse.

---

## §2. The Measure-Setting of the Decisive Thinkers and Poets for the Assessment of the Essence of Thinking and Poetizing

Nevertheless, we prefer to name these together: thinking and poetizing. They lie much closer together. In their difference, they have something in common that is not merely exhausted by the fact that both are human activities—as in the previous

---

2. [The original here reads: *Vergleichen und Vergleichen ist nicht überall das Gleiche.*—Trans.]

case. According to one conception familiar to modern thought, one could say that thinking and poetizing are "creative" activities, which does not apply to bike-riding, yet still does apply, for example, to architecture and painting.

Yet thinking and poetizing reveal an even closer relation [*Verwandtschaft*] than thinking and painting. Thinking and poetizing exist exclusively in the realm of language. Their works and only theirs are of a linguistic "nature."

But "thinking and poetizing," after all, are known to us in this naming that has somehow gathered them into one. "Thinkers and poets" belong together in an emphatic way for us. They are near to each other in a proximity that we can perhaps experience, if we know a few things about thinking and poetizing. Or do we only name thinkers and poets together because we are here following some habit that emerged at some point in time? So does the same [*das Gleiche*] in which thinking and poetizing resemble each other [*sich gleichen*], and the difference, in which they are dissimilar, remain indeterminate and vacillating?

Need this long-standing indeterminateness and vacillation disturb us? What is the point of comparing thinking and poetizing more clearly? Why should we compare them at all, and thus have a discussion "about" thinking and "about" poetizing? Does it not suffice if we simply follow the thinking of thinkers and emotionally "immerse" ourselves in the poetizing of the poets? But which ones among the thinkers and which ones among the poets should we follow? All of the historically known thinkers and poets? Or only ours? But are our thinkers and poets the ones that they are without the ancients and the older ones, without the thinkers and poets of the Greek age? Is there a standard [*Maß*] for measuring along with which thinkers we are allowed to think [*mitdenken*] and along with which poets we are allowed to poetize [*mitdichten*]? Or is this all left to the discretion and taste of the individual, to the trends of the day, to the tendencies of the age, to the rules of the institutions of education? Or is the burden of the correct choice decreased for us by the fact that the decisive [*maßgebenden*] thinkers and the decisive poets themselves provide the standard [*Maß*] according to which we grasp and assess [*ermessen*] the essence and the necessity of thinking and poetizing? The latter is presumably the case.

---

## §3. The Necessity of a Preparation for the Hearing of Thinking and Poetizing

But if this is the case, then how are we to hear and receive this standard [*Maß*], if we are inexperienced with what thinking is and with what poetizing is? Does our ear not then have to be perfectly and discriminately trained, and also have to be suitable for careful hearing [*Vernehmen*],[3] if thinkers and poets are to speak to us and if another claim is to meet us through them? How can we be the ones affected [*Betroffenen*], if we do not truly know what thinking is and what poetizing is? Knowing [*Wissen*] is not just the application of concepts, with whose help one could provide a definition on demand about what philosophy is and what poetry is. Here, knowing means the following: to be able to pursue and accompany the thinker by thinking and to pursue and accompany the poet by poetizing. The ability demands a permanence and a position. Wherever these are lacking, the voice of the thinkers and the poets can never meet [*treffen*] us; we can never be the ones affected [*Betroffenen*]. For, the shock [*Betroffenheit*] does not consist in a surge of emotions and mental excitement that is indeterminate and immediately fleeting. We are only affected and can only be affected if we can answer to the voice of the thinker and the poet, and that means to abide in the answer, or to learn to abide, or at the very least to be able to learn to abide. But that already requires some kind of knowledge of thinking and poetizing.

What help is it when, every semester, other thinkers and poets are presented to us so that they are forgotten during the next semester? What purpose does this all serve, if the historical presentation of thinkers and poets falls upon [those who

---

3. [*Vernehmen* (Old High German *farnëman*), which Heidegger uses here and I have rendered as "hearing," means "to become aware." It is important to emphasize the connection to *wahrnehmen* (perception) and *Vernunft* (reason), which, according to Herman Paul, is related etymologically to *vernehmen*.—Trans.]

are] unprepared? Just by the fact that we are "interested" in poets and thinkers, or demand them, or are even ready for them, does not mean that we are prepared.

We are barely aware of the fact that a preparation is necessary, and we think even less about what that entails. When I say "we," I do not only mean you, the audience, who are here and elsewhere at the mercy of an arbitrary offering of presentations about thinkers and poets. But I also mean those of us who are standing here and teaching; these first and foremost. Yet this is not an accusation. Not only is the authority lacking for this, but accusing and excusing would also be too little here. It is a matter of pointing out an already long-lasting failure whose type and whose origins, especially because they are older than we are, concern us in our essence by reaching over and beyond us. Therefore, we cannot immediately and willfully cast aside the absence [Ausbleiben] of the appropriate preparation for the hearing of thinking and poetizing.

Yet it is indeed direly necessary that we take note anew every day how confused and unreflective our relation to thinking and poetizing is. We take it as agreed that the cultivation of the vine and the harvest of grapes require a peculiar kind of knowledge and experience. At the same time one finds it normal to "deal" [»umgeht«][4] with the thinking of thinkers and the poetizing of poets according to one's own desires, arriving at them on the street or elsewhere, and appealing to one's impressions and experiences, as they come and go, provided that one reflects [besinnen] at all upon what is happening in this "handling" [»Umgang«] of thinking and of poetizing. As if one even could deal with [umgehen] the thinking of thinkers or the poetizing of poets, or were allowed to.

Prior to everything else, there is a dire need that we first reflect on the lack of reflection [Besinnungslose] in this dealing. It is already sufficient if we become reflective [besinnlich] upon the intrusive indifference, due to which we pass by the preparation for thinking and poetizing.

---

4. [Heidegger most likely puts the verb umgehen in quotes to emphasize the ambiguity of the verb. Umgehen can mean "to handle," "deal with," but also can mean "to circle around something" with the intention of avoiding it.—Trans.]

If we reflect on this long-standing unreflective condition of
those unprepared for the hearing of the thinker and of the poet;
if we reflect in this way, then the title "thinking and poetizing"
will possibly address us differently; if we also recall [*entsinnen*]
that we are the people of thinkers and poets, then we can assess
[*ermessen*] with some intimation how far away we still stand
from the gathering of our own essence. It is as if an unimagi-
nable destiny has completely alienated us from this gathering.

"Thinking and Poetizing," the title for a perhaps merely indifferent comparison of thinking and poetizing, in which we
could discuss erudite matters about the relationship between
philosophy and poetry; "Thinking and Poetizing," the indication of an inevitable reflection [*Besinnung*], inevitable when
we hearken to the most silent course [*Gang*] of the concealed
history of the West and by doing so experience that we can
only deny this course if we have already renounced the future
of Western history.

--------

### §4. Reflection on Thinking and Poetizing
### and Their Relationship.
### The Question-Worthy as the Standard for
### Contemplation

Let us reflect [*besinnen*]; let us reflect on thinking and poetizing. How could we do this other than by contemplating [*nachsinnen*] about thinking, whatever it may be, and about poetizing, whatever it may be, and about the relationship of the two?
What is thinking? Can we just freely think up the answer?
What is poetizing? Can we just freely fantasize [*erdichten*] the
answer? With such an approach, we would soon fall victim to
a baseless arbitrariness. Yet where is there a measure [*Maß*]
here, with which we can assess [*ermessen*] the essence of thinking and the essence of poetizing? If there is a measure here,
who provides it? Where and how do we find the measure-setting [*Mas-Gebende*] for our contemplation?
All real reflection [*Besinnen*], with each of its steps, immediately progresses deeper into the realm of the question-worthy [*Fragwürdigen*]. The latter is different than what is merely
dubious [*Fragliche*], which occurs in many forms. It appears as

the uncertain, as the undecided, and as the unexplained.
What is merely dubious evades us, or more precisely, it itself
always remains, but does so in such a way that it withdraws
and withholds something from us and thus leaves us behind.
What is merely dubious thus also simply becomes what we, by
ourselves, leave behind. After all, it is precisely dubious, i.e.,
always questionable, but not necessarily to be questioned.

The question-worthy [Fragwürdige] stands in opposition to
the merely dubious, and taken literally, "the word" means that
which is worthy of questioning [was der Befragung würdig ist].
Yet we use the words "question-worthy" in a belittling sense. In
this sense, it means the doubtful, the unreliable, or even the
corrupted, and thus what is unworthy. This is precisely what
language calls the question-worthy, so it is something worthy.
But with this usage of the word, we completely forget that we
are talking about dignity and what is worthy. [What a] strange
forgetfulness, and an even stranger prevalence of language!

However, we ourselves can see from this common use of the
term "question-worthy" that we mean something else by it, something that concerns us and makes us involved, even when we
hold it away from us. The merely dubious does not affect us. The
question-worthy, on the other hand, the word now taken literally, opens itself up to us in its dignity, which demands from us
that we correspond to it, i.e., that we dignify it by questioning.

But is questioning not rather an intrusion of a willing that,
merely for itself and by itself, wants to arrogate knowledge to
itself? Questioning—is it a way of preserving [wahren] for each
worthy [thing] its dignity? Is questioning, even when it avoids
intrusion and even if it is completely hidden, not always a dis-
regard of dignity?

Dignifying is more akin to recognizing, simply letting the
dignity speak for itself and from itself, and therefore not
speaking and thus not questioning. How, then, can questioning take over something like dignifying as the preservation of
dignity? At the most, there would have to be something whose
ownmost dignity, as it were, lies in the majesty [Hoheit] that is
"contemplative" and "reflective" in itself. The human could
conform to and adequately dignify this height [Hohen] and its
dignity solely by contemplating the height that is contemplative in itself.

A late revision [*Umdichtung*] of the poem "The Blind Singer," "Chiron," begins:[5]

Wo bist du, Nachdenkliches! das immer muß
Zur Seite gehn, zu Zeiten, wo bist du, Licht?

Where are you, the Contemplative! What always must
depart, at times, where are you, Light?

The light, the brightness, is the contemplative; Hölderlin capitalizes "Contemplative" so that we have to say that the contemplative is the light. The light comes "advising, for the sake of the heart." The high watch [*Warte*] of the brightness, and this itself, is fundamentally so clear [*licht*] that humans—not even gods—could ever see it directly. This indicates that the clear [*das Lichte*] as such conceals itself. The clear clears itself out of its clearing [*Lichtung*], such that this clearing is simultaneously concealment and constantly pursues and contemplates this. The contemplative is that in which the height of the majesty that reposes itself, its dignity, lies.

Contemplation is the incipient, beginning questioning that remains unexpressed for a long time and stays removed from every loud inquiry and interrogation in which humans insist on their own power. Contemplation not only reluctantly dignifies the height that is contemplative in itself; rather, contemplation is a dignifying that first uncovers the concealed dignity of that which thought would like to encounter on its way. Yet reflection [*Besinnen*] is only real if it emerges from contemplation [*Nachsinnen*] and solely serves it by abiding in it. Therefore we may say: All real reflection arrives in the realm of the question-worthy instantly and with every step. Stated more adequately, reflection already *is* in this realm. The question-worthy is what is decisive [*Maßgebende*] for contemplation. The question-worthy, that is first dignified in contemplative questioning, renders [its own] questions for reflection that are heavier from their own weight than everything dubious and the questions that are oriented toward it.

One characteristic of the questions that emerge from the question-worthy itself consists in the fact that they continually

---

5. F. Hölderlin, *Sämtliche Werke* (ed. Hellingrath), vol. IV, p. 65.

return into themselves and are thus not to be answered in the usual way. The posing of these questions encounters peculiar difficulties that contemplation must not avoid because they are perhaps characteristics of the proper dignity of the question-worthy, provided that thinking, whatever it may be, and given that poetizing, whatever it may be, belong to the question-worthy; the same goes for the relation between thinking and poetizing, which is named by the ambiguous and thus initially meaningless "and."

What difficulties present themselves to contemplation here? We will name two now and discuss them.

The first difficulty concerns the teaching of that from which we could even see what thinking and poetizing are.

The second difficulty appears insofar as we, contemplating thinking and poetizing as contemplators, already stand by thinking on the one side of the relationship between thinking and poetizing, such that everything to be said is one-sided in advance.

# SUPPLEMENTS

## Second Version of the Review:
### Introduction to Philosophy—Thinking and Poetizing[1]

Philosophy is the thinking of thinkers. They think that which is, being, insofar as it determines beings. For a long time, and today still, that which comes to presence [das Anwesende], the present, counts for Western thinking as that which is. But even that which is in the process of arriving [das Kommende] already is in its arriving. That which was [das Gewesene] also still is, insofar as it comes to presence and passes over us. Future and origin approach each other. In this facing approach, future and origin surpass each other alternatively in different expanses. What is present [das Gegenwärtige] first emerges from out of the facing approach of the future and the origin. [What is present] is that which appears to leap out of the facing approach and spread itself open for itself, and which makes it seem as if what is present were all that exists, while that which was is *no* longer and that which is to come is *not* yet—thus at each point they do not exist. What is present only exists as the alternating transition of what is to come into what was and of what was into what is to come. Therefore, every present moment is an ambiguous ambiguity. If we only search in the present for that which *is,* we will never find it, because what is present remains ambiguous, and this ambiguity stems directly from what exceeds the present and exists more so [eher] than does the present.

---

1. Important material about history and historiography and technology. [A review of GA 50, pp. 90-101.—Ed.]

Thinkers think that which is. Their thinking is *thinking*, the word is strictly used for them. Insofar as historical humans think of the future from out of the origin and of the origin from out of the future, and thus reflectively [*andenkend*] think what is present, humans continually think that which is. The historical human thinks. For this reason, there are times of impoverished thought and thoughtlessness in history. The historical human thinks. The human philosophizes. The historical human stands in philosophy. Therefore, we can also not first be introduced "to" philosophy. Nevertheless, a guide is necessary in order for historical humans to become at home and to first learn authentic dwelling where they already sojourn, however ineptly and obliviously.

Historical humans think historically, i.e., from out of what has been sent into the appropriate that sends itself to the human. Thinking historically [*geschichtlich*] is something essentially different than thinking historiographically [*historisch*].[2] Historiography [*Historie*] thinks, if its mode of presentation may even be called that, unhistorically. Historiography necessarily ignores what is destined [*Geschickhafte*] and only speaks cursorily and thoughtlessly of destiny [*Schicksal*]. For historiography assumes that history [*Geschichte*] is a series of results, i.e., the sequential course of causes and effects. It calculates according to these. Historiographical portrayals of the past are blueprints of procedures and developments, of progression and failure, of victories and losses, of influences and impacts. Historiography computes history and calculates with it. Calculating is the fundamental trait of technology. Historiography is a mode of technical representation that seizes history in the claws of technology and of its own calculation. Modern historiography, like modern natural science, emerged from modern technology. Thus, if modern technology first begins in our century to unveil its heretofore concealed essence, an essence that does not consist at all in the

2. [In the following passage Heidegger will distinguish *Historie* from *Geschichte*, both of which translate into English as "history." Heidegger's critique of *Historie* parallels what we call "historiography" in English, and has been translated as that. Additionally, *Geschichte* comes from the verb *geschehen*, "that which has happened," and resembles, although not etymologically, the German word for destiny, *Geschick*. —Trans.]

manufacture of machines, then from an essentially historical perspective it precedes modern natural science as its destiny. Modern technology is not at all merely the application of modern natural science to the manufacture of machines and devices; rather, from its beginning modern natural science is in its essence the technical assault on nature and its conquest [*Eroberung*]. The twentieth century, in which the age of modernity will most likely fulfill itself—not that it will end—can only be, in fact must therefore be, the age of technology, because this is the originary and thus long-concealed destiny of modernity. As historiography, along with natural science, has the same essential origin in technology, and since modern science is itself a kind of technology, the sciences can and must immediately be mobilized in today's nations.

Historical humans think, and when humans genuinely think, i.e., insofar as they themselves are the property of destiny, they think historically. Humans think reflectively on the origin and the future and on both in their facing approach [*Entgegenkunft*]. To think something that goes beyond us and spreads over us, and especially to think something coming toward us and befitting *us*, is a comportment that remains fundamentally different from recalculating the past's aftereffects and from the planning calculation of the present's influences and probable results.

If philosophy is genuine thinking, and thinking thinks historically, then philosophy thinks historically. Indeed, it only thinks historically—but never historiographically [*historisch*]. Yet as soon as a historian not merely calculates historiographically [*historisch*] but also thinks, i.e., thinks historically, then he has already begun to philosophize.

The introduction to philosophy is the guiding of initially inept thinking to the careful thinking of that which is. This circumspection of thinking unfolds in such as way that remembrance becomes more reflective and such that thinking becomes more historical.

Many paths stand open for a guide to thinking; all, of course, are necessarily paths of the experience of history.

Review of pp. 105ff.
(Nietzsche. On the Relationship between
Thinking and Poetizing)

Instead of maintaining general discussions "about" thinking
and poetizing, we are attempting to think along with Nietzsche, the poetizing thinker, and to poetize along with Hölderlin, the thoughtful poet. However, even after this clarification
by names, the path of our reflection [*Besinnung*] remains ex-
posed to further misinterpretations. If we wanted to first
sweep all these out of the way, we would never get under way.
It is also certainly not advisable to shove the imposing misinterpretations aside and to set off on the path in the hope that
everything obscure would become clear on its own along the
way. The questions and concerns that have emerged in the
meantime could be drawn together with two remarks. One
group of questions concerns Nietzsche, the poet; the other
concerns Nietzsche's relationship to Hölderlin.

We do not see Nietzsche as the poetizing thinker for the
reason that "poems" can be found scattered in his texts and
notebooks, and because the work *Thus Spoke Zarathustra* makes
the definite impression of a poetic style with its language and
form. We can only understand why this is named as it is when
we know to what extent and in what sense poetizing belongs
to Nietzsche's thinking. What first of all remains necessary is
to contemplate Nietzsche's thinking. In fact, Nietzsche's own
statements concerning poetizing and poetry only say something when we grasp them from out of his thinking, e.g., the
following note from the summer of 1885:

> Germany has only produced one poet, besides Goethe: that is
> Heinrich Heine—and he was a Jew on top of that . . . (vol. XIV,
> no. 334, p. 173)

This note casts an unusual light on the poet Goethe. Goethe—
Heine, "the" poet of Germany. Where is Hölderlin, to just
name this one, since we are placing him together with Nietzsche? Did Nietzsche not even know Hölderlin's poetry?

## Second Version of the Manuscript pp. 4-5:
*On Thinking and Poetizing. Considerations for the Lecture*[3]
(Preliminary Questions for the Reflection on
Thinking and Poetizing)

Let us reflect, let us reflect on thinking and poetizing. How could we do this other than by contemplating [*nachsinnen*] thinking and what it might be, by contemplating poetizing and what it might be, and finally by contemplating the relationship of the two?

What is thinking? Can we just freely think up an answer? What is poetizing? Can we just freely fantasize an answer? With such an approach, we would have to fall victim to a baseless arbitrariness. But if there is to be no arbitrariness, where is there a measure [*Maß*] with which we can ascertain the essence of thinking and the essence of poetizing? If there is a measure here, who provides it? Where and how do we find the standard measure-setting [*Maß-Gebende*] for our contemplation that reflects on thinking and poetizing?

Yet there is a simple method by which we can expose the questions just now brought forward as artificially constructed questions. After all, we know the long and rich history of Western thinking and its thinkers. What we do not know right away, we can familiarize ourselves with at any time, with the help of historiographical research of the history of thinking. There we are presented with the thinking of particular thinkers among the Greeks; we follow the sequence of the thinkers of modernity. If we do not limit ourselves to the characterization of a single thinker and his thinking, but rather compare several thinkers and their thinking, we are also protected against unevenly abiding by one single thinker, e.g., against judging all philosophizing according to Kant's philosophy and presenting only Kant's thinking as thinking *as such*. If we indeed comparatively review the entire history of thinking from Thales to Nietzsche, then the general idea almost immediately occurs to us on its own of what the thinking of thinkers could be. The same applies for the determination of what poetizing might be. Literary-historiographical research provides us diverse means

---

3. [Cf. GA 50, pp. 142ff.—Ed.]

by which to learn the poetizing of poets from Homer to Rilke, and to determine through comparative consideration what poetizing in general might be. If we then finally compare the general essence of thinking and poetizing, then what is the same and different in thinking and poetizing must become obvious. That is the most natural way for a reflection [*Besinnung*] on thinking and poetizing.

Anyone will surely admit that this historiographical comparative constellation [*Durchmusterung*] of the entire history of thinking and poetizing surpasses the ability of an individual human. This task is impossible in a practical sense. This might also be the reason why we always only have indeterminate and alternating ideas about thinking and poetizing at our disposal.

But let us just once suppose that the history of thinking, as well as the history of poetizing, could be assessed in its fundamental traits and taken as the basis for a comparative consideration—then the question would be permitted of how the historiographical presentations of the history of thinking and poetizing know which thinking and which poetizing better reveal the fundamental traits of thinking and poetizing. But how are we to differentiate and conclude what belongs to the history of thinking and what belongs to the history of poetizing, if we do not at first already know what thinking is and what poetizing is, and what constitutes their difference? The vast undertaking that comparatively and historiographically traces the history of thinking as well as the history of poetizing in order to then again compare both "histories," could not even make progress if it were not already known what thinking is, what poetizing is, and what their difference is. But if one already previously requires that which the historiographical comparisons should first provide as a result, then why the entire undertaking?

If one already imports an idea of thinking and poetizing, from where does one draw these ideas, from where do they have their authority [*Maßgeblich*] that they demand whenever they serve as introductions for historiographical evaluation? These questions are old and return whenever we ask what this or that might be. They concern every mode of presenting things, every way of experience, and every human relation to what encounters the human. What humans encounter, and what concerns humans themselves, does not happen to them and does not simply fall into humans like rain into the gutter. What encounters humans, they also respond to, even where and when they apparently comport themselves indifferently and passively toward that which they encounter. Humans respond to that which encounters them—therefore we can also say: That which encounters shows itself each and every time in a determined light. That which encounters comes each and every time from out of a determined region that it never abandons even once it arrives. That everything coming to presence, and everything coming and going along with it, always appears in a determined and determining light, the thinker Plato—propelled by his teacher Socrates—truly saw and thought this out for the first time, and what is decisive is that he attempted to explain this. The explanation he gave is the doctrine of the "ideas"—a doctrine that ever since has dominated the entire thinking of the West. According to this doctrine of ideas, we also speak of what was just mentioned in the following way: In order to find such a thing as "thinking" and "poetizing" within history, and to recognize them as what they are called, we have to already have an "idea" of "thinking" and an "idea" of "poetizing." Without the "ideas" nothing could encounter the human. Without the ideas, humans could also not respond to that which encounters them. But what are the "ideas?" Where do they have their origin? From where do they hold their validity? Plato already asked these questions, and since then they are still repeatedly asked in some way. Even today, argumentations about and conceptions of the world still divide themselves according to the interpretations of the ideas, of the conceptual [*Ideellen*], and of the ideal [*Idealen*]. "Materialism," which teaches that the ideas and all ideals are only subsequent products of particular economic-technical circumstances or life processes, could not be the materialism that it is without the basis of the ideas. Every action and every passion of modern humanity is grounded in an expressed or unexpressed assumption of the ideas, without knowing what this assumption itself is. The fact of all facts is that the ideas are assumed in everything. [This fact] can also be paraphrased as follows: The ideas are that which lie above the sensible world as the conceptual. Let us designate the sensible as the physical . . .

### Two Fragmentary Versions of Manuscript p. 12[4]

#### a) First Fragmentary Version

Yet we are not inquiring into the empty and indeterminate. We are asking about the poetizing thinking of Nietzsche's metaphysics, in which is thought what now is, namely beings in their being. What kind of essence does this being of beings, which now is, reveal? What and how are beings that concern us in our heart and blood, our bones and marrow, which concern us in spirit and from the soul, whether we truly want to have them or not, whether we avoid them or oppose them, whether we are always following a few occurrences among beings and remain dependent on the immediately approaching conditions of beings impinging upon us, or if we always still and always only . . .

#### b) Second Fragmentary Version

With such reflection, even if we come across important questions, we nevertheless run the risk that, inquiring into the indeterminate and empty, we are just "speculating" "about" thinking and poetizing. Questioning is not fulfilled as long as it is rampant and loses the trace, or cannot even first find it. Even the most important questions are only real, i.e., questions that emerged according to their measure, if they are asked in the *single* free-space [*Spielraum*] of the *single* question, which is: What now is? That is the question of thinking, of thinking in every case. "Now" always means the respective time of those who say "now." "Now" means our time, the time in which we belong. The time in which we belong is the time in which it is time for us; the time in which we may not neglect it. Which "it"?

That on which everything depends: the entirety that arrives and belongs to us: being. We belong in our time if it becomes *time* for us according to this time—if we think what now is. It is time for us, that means that time reaches over beyond us and makes use of us from its expanse, so that we do not neglect ourselves. The "now," our time, is the far-reaching time. The time that speeds *over* us but that thus also reaches beyond *us* is precisely the modern era. Historically calculating—.

---

4. [Cf. GA 50, pp. 128ff.—Ed.]

The "now" does not only mean the foregrounded moment of time of current world events. The "now" means this twentieth century and the three centuries prior to it. These are the past centuries for historiographical consideration. But for the historical experience they still *are* now, possibly are now for the first time.

_____

### Notes to the Lecture:
*Introduction to Philosophy—Thinking and Poetizing*[5]

*Thinking and Poetizing*—each time a meditation [*Sinnen*], each time a saying: the reflective word. The thinkers and poets, the ones who reflectively speak and the ones who verbally reflect.

*Dionysus* [is] the unconditional yes to the being of beings; that in the totality of beings, everything redeems and affirms itself; nothing is forbidden any longer—except for weakness; strength's urge to action. This yes—the Dionysian. Dionysus—as the name of the faith in the yes to the will to will.

*Will to will.* The highest one is called—being against the deepest despondency [*Schwermut*]. Over-pride [*Über-mut*] of the over-human, cf. vol. XII, pp. 397, 401.

*The to-be-poetized figure of Zarathustra* [is] metaphysically the single possibility of replying to the still-concealed fact that being *needs* the human essence.

In the completion this emerges in the most extreme indefiniteness. Appropriating in this way, the appropriative event lasts as expropriation.

Behind the will to power stands the fear of the nothing, which stands before the will as that which is not really knowable by it, but solely what is willed.

The eternal return of the same and *the same.* The same and "logic," cf. *Die fröhliche Wissenschaft,* no. 111. The doctrine of the eternal return, cf. vol. XIV, pp. 264, 267.

5. [GA 50, pp. 156-60.—Trans.]

## The Eternal Return of the Same

The eternal return of the same and the view into the undetermined emptiness of homogeneity of the mere "always again." Thus beyond progress, but also beyond the finite coming to an end. One thing applies: the will wills and can will its willing. Where and how is the "again"—*iterum*—necessary? Precisely never, at any time. The identical—"the same" [*»Das Gleiche«*] and the "same" [*»Selbe«*].

The evasion of the inevitable essence of being into which the will to power has to will itself, and that means that in the willing of the eternal return of the same, it first wills itself *in the highest absolute* condition (i.e., the condition completely conditioned by the will to power itself). In the eternal return [is] the absolute self-willing of the will to power. The eternal return of the same as the will to will.

The thought of the eternal return of the same: "*A prophecy.*"

1. *Pre*-diction—forecast—prognostication—anticipation—pre-willing—"a prophecy," (vol. XVI, p. 413). The greatest, longest will. The actual work in the will to will that wills that which still conditions the will to power as the *absolute*—conditioning itself. "*Forward*"-willing belongs to the will as command: anticipation and infringement.

2. And to say what is *true* of beings—what the will to power is as being. *The interpretation of being.* But values [are] being as the will to will. Will—subjectivity; *actualitas*—ἐνέϱγεια; presence—οὐσία: the constant presence as will is only as the will to will.

*The nothing of being* (in the metaphysical sense—οὐσία—φύσις). The goallessness of the will to power itself—that "only" wills itself. *The nothing of being as being.* Here the concealed "return" that the nothing still wills and must will into being—so immense is the will. "The nothing"—the mere negative of beings—the emptiness—what is negated in the bright no. The *nothing*—as the negative of goallessness, this as the single goal, the affirmed nothing.

The radical nihilist, cf. *Der Wille zur Macht*, no. 25, 1887: "Goallessness in itself" the *sought-after* goal, i.e., to think the will to power in its essence as being.

The most extreme—*willing the nothing in order to will.* The most extreme nihilism and the most radical are the same, not a reversal, but??—, rather the highest uprising of the *animal rationale* at the highest peak of the essence of the will as the will to will. This uprising is an "over and beyond itself" of the previous human, not in the direction of the previous moral transcendence, but instead far beyond itself and the previous not-yet into its *most extremely thought form.*

The yes to the eternal return of the same, to absolute truth, the constancy of being still not grounded in its truth in the sense of *constant presence* (cf. *Der Wille zur Macht,* vol. XV, no. 1061); this in the most extreme figure of the will to will (cf. ibid., no. 1041).

The eternal return of the same [is] not determined and calculated for beings by a "description" or an "explanation"; rather, just as the entire truth of beings: ὑπόθεσις, says Plato. But what is that?

The will to power is what is "poetized" in the book; this is οὐσία, *actualitas,* objectivity.

The most extreme form of nihilism!—to what extent is the nothing willed here? To experience the *absolute nothing* (of what?—*of what beings?*); having willed and in this willing is still the self-willing-itself.

*"The recurrence"—the return—without history;* the empty *"iteration"* of the empty circle. *Against* the *univocity* of metaphysical time—and yet "time," but not experienced in its essence as *truth.* The *will to power* as the *will to will*—therein [is] the circling, *circulus.*

Fear "behind" the will to power? "Behind"; the *nothing* never stands *facing* [the will to power]; being afraid of this as a must, the will *affirms* it and calls that its freedom.

The Will to Power—the Eternal Return of the Same

The supporting and determinative [element] of his thinking is the thought that Nietzsche himself calls "the thought of thoughts." That is the thought of the eternal return of the same. And "the will to power"? Is this not the fundamental trait of beings? Is not the thought of the will to power the thought of thoughts?—

With the eternal return of the same, the homelessness of the uprising experienced by Nietzsche is thought in the will to power as "the home."—The most extreme homelessness is achieved in this [home]; it corresponds, although unknowingly and unrecognizable in its essence for metaphysical thinking, to being's final abandonment of beings and being's forgetfulness of the human essence.

*Return* as irreparable, unmodified monotony of what has once happened, unhistorical, thing-like; the constancy through mere reiteration, i.e., the constancy as *will to power* (in general as a prerequisite for *becoming*), so that the will can be a will in such a way that what enables it as a will, i.e., gives it constancy, is itself such that it can only be thought—and heard as being— in the most decisive, absolute will to mastery.

*The thought of thoughts*, the thought of the eternal return of the same, is the thought of absolute mastery, not only over beings but over being.

How the will to power still returned in the thinking of that which enables it itself. How the *will to power* wills itself here to the greatest extent, and how it itself is. Thus not to take the relation of the will to power and the eternal return of the same externally.

# Appendix to *Nietzsche's Metaphysics*

## Notes to *Nietzsche's Metaphysics*[6]

This thinking will not become real by being transferred into a practice as philosophy; rather, thinking as thinking of being and, i.e., from out of being, is that which appears in advance from out of the same being among beings themselves.

On the determination of the essence of metaphysics, cf. the note about the history of the concept of metaphysics (1932). Essence of metaphysics out of the truth of being.

The four determinations: *essentia, existentia,* history, the human essence—united in the fifth: the truth of beings as such. Metaphysics knows only a few constitutive parts of itself in its interpretation, but not the essential unity from beyng [*Seyn*].[7]

Nietzsche's thought of *"justice"* and "Christian" metaphysics. Cf. *justice and the just in* Meister Eckhart;—*iustitia* and *certitudo.*

"Justice"—its concealed essence: the totality of the truth of beings as such, insofar as being is the will to power as absolute subjectivity.

---

6. [GA 50, pp. 83-87.—Trans.]

7. [Heidegger's return to the archaic spelling of *Sein* as *Seyn* corresponds to his linguistic attempt to cross over the history of metaphysics to a more originary experience of being that is here translated as "beyng," an Old English variation of "being."—Trans.]

Subjectivity and *certitudo:* Descartes; ⎫
*ego cogito, res cogitans, mens.*                    ⎬ Modernity, beginning
*Iustificatio, iustitia*—Luther.                  ⎭
*Iustitia* and *ordo mentium*—Leibniz.

*Quid iuris*—the way of questioning for Kant's transcendental deduction as the self-certainty of subjectivity.

*Certitudo*—certitude—value; value assessment—more fundamental; "Justice" more fundamental than certainty. The connection with *rectitudo*, as this is still in *certitudo*, altered but preserved by *perceptio* and *repraesentatio*. Why Nietzsche himself is unable to think either the essence of truth of certainty, or even that of justice. The thought of values blocks everything. The final testimony of the forgetfulness of being.

A question introduces the following consideration. This means: We attempt to bring, and do not deliver, an answer. But asking . . . : point to where the answer could arrive. But is the question important? Whether it is or not emerges out of itself. Pointing in the direction in which Nietzsche's thinking accomplishes the completion of metaphysics.

***

## Who Is Zarathustra?
### A Confrontation with Nietzsche

Let us take the word "confrontation" literally. We are attempting to set Nietzsche's thinking and our thinking apart from one another and over against one another; but thoughtfully, not comparatively.

His thinking: what Nietzsche thought. Our thinking: what is worthy of thought for us. The one and the other *from* one another; they are still within each other—not in the sense of two standpoints being tangled with one another; not as if our thinking had flowed out of Nietzsche's. No thinking emerges out of another, but instead only out of its to-be-thought; nevertheless, [there is] no thinking without what precedes it—the predecessors.

Nietzsche is the name for an age: the epoch of the development and installation of the mastery of the human over the earth. The human as the subject of production. The earth as the core area of the objectivity of world use: the forgetfulness of beyng, the remoteness of history, neglect; humans and thinking; thinking and language; thinking in the age of neglect; that which has been spoken of this thinking: *Thus Spoke Zarathustra.*

Who is Zarathustra?—What is his language like?—What is he within it?

## Nietzsche's *Thus Spoke Zarathustra*

The *interpretation:* to respond so essentially to a matter that Nietzsche's word might remain untouched and resound purely from this matter. But this matter is the "essence" of the human insofar as it is given over to the question of the world.

Yet this essence still remains concealed; concealed because it [is] refused; refused in the way of the omission in the completed subjectivity of the self-producing will to unstable constancy. The ultimate neglect of the human essence in the appearance of the unbounded performance of order and the mere creation of its own conditions. But the order is the controllability.

The adequately thoughtful interpretation is achieved where its form is absent.

The answer to the question who Zarathustra is cannot be given with a sentence, and also not with several sentences; instead, [it is] only [given] in an encounter with Zarathustra. What Zarathustra is determines what this encounter consists of. We experience who Zarathustra is in the encounter.

The circle is closed. A circle is here in advance. We must go around through it. But how will we arrive within the circle? We are already in it. But we are not gleaning any knowledge from it. Not only we here, but the human of today does not know the circle; and not only modern humans but also their age, and also the age before this one, do not know the circle. And yet they were also already inside it.

In his own way, and in another style, Nietzsche knew about it. Every creative one at most seeks his work elevated in the horizon that this work reveals. [The creative one] never experiences what first occurs in the work. Within this boundary lies the greatness of the creator.

The greatest among them are those in whose work the boundary simply becomes unavoidable, i.e., decided to the utmost in such a way that the creator purely remains in its boundary and knows it without naming it.

Who is Zarathustra? He is the teacher of the eternal return of the same. As this teacher he teaches the *Übermensch;* he is not yet this himself. His speeches begin with this doctrine, not as if he first progresses from the doctrine of the *Übermensch* to the doctrine of the eternal return, but because this is the first thing to be taught, and from there the last to be said; he is silent for a long time about that which he knows.

Wherein is the cohesion of both doctrines grounded? In what respect does Nietzsche search and think this cohesion?

The *Übermensch* is the meaning of the earth. The earth as what is guarded by the *Übermensch.* The *Übermensch:* the human to whom the earth be entrusted.

What is the *earth?*—Earth and conquest of the earth; the destruction—the crime upon the earth.

What is this: to teach the *Übermensch*? To say who it is and how it is: letting learn—to be led into its essence.

To learn: to experience the danger.

---

## Return and *Übermensch*

Why and how do the eternal return of the same and the *Übermensch* belong together? Why and how does an (un-thought) cohesion immediately appear in Nietzsche's metaphysics? Why can the doctrine of the (eternal) return of the same neither be *proved nor* disproved? What kind of "doctrine" is this? *Projection* of the being of beings. From where and how?

---

## Eternal Return of the Same and *Übermensch*

Nietzsche thinks more clearly, yet without experiencing it in its essence, the essence of the human from being (cf. vol. XII, pp. 398, 400-401). Thinking is pushed into this relation in the most extreme neglect, without being able to think it, neither the relation itself nor that wherein the itself is: *world*. Rather the relation remains involved in the most extreme subjectivity: the hammer. Eternal return of the same as "doctrine" and "thought," instead of thinking—event-like;—"the hammer."

---

## *Zarathustra's* Preface

The beginning: the sun—the cave (high in the mountains); completely different than for Plato and *yet* the *same*. But closer to the turn; yet, thought symbolically, equally distant and equally near. But: the *subjectivity* of the human and its role in (beyng) as objectivity.

To what extent is thinking confrontation? It takes over the un-thought. It is only capable of this when it is trusted by what is to be thought. To confront: thinking sets itself apart from thinking. Only this way is one capable of encountering the other. Only as such is there oppositional response. In this way thinking liberates itself [*befreyt sich*] from the "anti" of antagonism—in the belonging to the same.

The further the separation, the more abiding the nearness.

The more lingering the nearness, the more decisive is the distance.

The further away what is near, the more essential [*wesend*] what has been.

# LECTURE ANNOUNCEMENTS:
## TRANSCRIPTIONS AND FACSIMILES

Martin Heidegger's handwritten announcements, reproduced below as a facsimile, were posted on the notice board as the final lecture and seminar announcements at the University of Freiburg and were singed and charred after the bombing attack on Freiburg on 27 November 1944. The announcements were salvaged by an unknown person. Much later they came into the possession of Rauser, the Mayor of Messkirch, from an older married couple from the surrounding area of Messkirch. Rauser gave them to the Messkirch Martin Heidegger Archive on 9 September 1989. The handwriting was transcribed for improved legibility and has been reduced by about twenty percent.—Ed.

---

### Transcriptions of the Facsimiles

#### W.S. 1944/45

1. *Introduction to Philosophy*
   (Thinking & Poetizing)
   One hour; Thurs. 5-6 pm, Lecture Hall 90.

2. *Exercises for Advanced [Students];*
   Two hours, according to appointment;
   Preliminary meeting on Friday, Nov. 10th, 6 pm,
   in the Philosophy Seminar room.

3. *Colloquium for War Veterans*

What is Science?
Preliminary meeting on Mon. Nov. 13, 6 pm,
Lecture Hall 57.

*Office Hours:* Thursday following the lecture
    in the Director's Room in the Philosophy Seminar room.

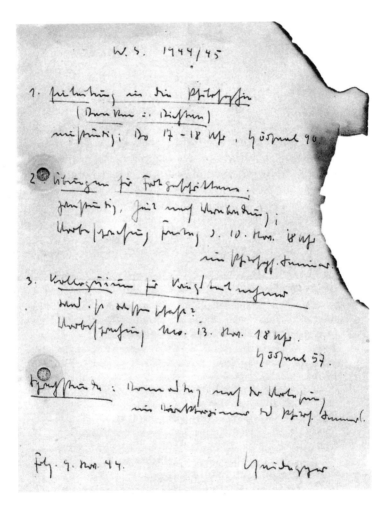

Frbg. 9. Nov. 44                                                    Heidegger

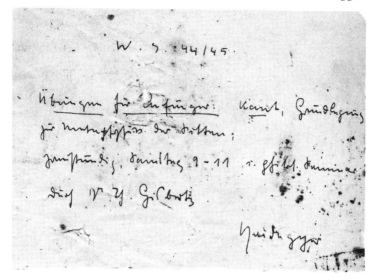

W.S. 44/45

*Exercises for Beginners: Kant,* Groundwork
of the Metaphysics of Morals;
Two hours, Saturday 9–11 am, Philosophy Seminar room
with Dr. Th. Gisbertz.

Heidegger

# Editor's Afterword

According to Martin Heidegger's wishes, *Gesamtausgabe* 50 combines two lecture manuscripts. Heidegger had announced his course for the Winter Semester 1941-1942 under the title "Nietzsche's Metaphysics," but instead selected the lecture "Hölderlin's Hymne 'Andenken'" (now GA 52) instead of this one. Heidegger himself dates the original text of the former as August 1940; a revision was made in September 1940, and two reviews took place in October and December of the same year.

This edition is based on the handwritten version of the last revision, which deviates in minor respects from the version published by Neske in *Nietzsche II* (Pfullingen, 1961).[1] These deviations probably stem from the preparation of the printed manuscript in 1961. The *lecture* editions appear in the second division of the *Gesamtausgabe* of Martin Heidegger's writings. Marginal notes from the handwritten, revised versions are taken into consideration in the footnotes. These marginal notes have been identified and collated by Dr. Hartmut Tietjen and me. Fritz Heidegger had managed the transcription of this lecture record. Naturally, the structure of the manuscript as an introduction and five chapters, just as Heidegger himself planned it according to the five fundamental words of Nietzsche's metaphysics, has been preserved. Here, a sixth chapter is dedicated to the overview of the five fundamental words

---

1. [The editor's comments in this and the following paragraph refer to the lecture *Nietzsche's Metaphysics*, which appears alongside *Introduction to Philosophy—Thinking and Poetizing* in GA 50 but is not translated in the present volume.—Trans.]

along with the metaphysics of the will to power, for which Heidegger reserved a concluding section.

The volumes *Nietzsche I* and *Nietzsche II* from 1961 will appear again within division I of the *Gesamtausgabe*—exempt from typos but otherwise unchanged—as volumes 6.1 and 6.2. Volume 6.2 will thus also contain "Nietzsche's Metaphysics," in its 1961 form. The appendix to this lecture contains a selection of notes on Heidegger's Nietzsche-lectures.[2] These handwritten reflections were transcribed and collated by Dr. Hartmut Tietjen and me.

The second text of volume 50, with the title "Introduction to Philosophy: Thinking and Poetizing," is the lecture from the winter semester 1944–1945, which was cancelled after the second session. This, Heidegger's last publicly delivered lecture as a tenured professor, could not be continued because he was drafted into the *Volkssturm*. The "Considerations for the Lecture" are printed here in conjunction with the lecture text.[3]

When Heidegger began the preparation of the *Gesamtausgabe* with the help of Dr. Friedrich-Wilhelm von Hermann in the fall of 1973, he decided that this lecture should be published in conjunction with his last Nietzsche-lecture, i.e., in conjunction with "Nietzsche's Metaphysics," due to the thematic relation; due to its brevity, it would not have sufficed for a single volume.

Fritz Heidegger had prepared the typescript transcription for this lecture manuscript as well.

The appendix combines short texts of different kinds, which all have the thematic content of thinking and poetizing: second versions of pages, a review, as well as notes.[4]

For the work on this edition, Dr. Friedrich-Wilhelm von Hermann and Dr. Hartmut Tietjen were by my side once again with advice and energetic assistance. They deserve my warm thanks. Doctoral candidate Mark Michalski and Dr. Irmgard Jaeger were very helpful in the proofreading process. I would like to thank them for their assistance as well.

Petra Jaeger

2.  [These notes appear in the present volume as "Appendix to *Nietzsche's Metaphysics.*"—Trans.]
3.  [Heidegger's "Considerations for the Lecture" are translated in the section titled "Supplements."—Trans.]
4.  [This material is translated here as "Supplements."—Trans.]